APPROACHING JOB

CASCADE COMPANIONS

The Christian theological tradition provides an embarrassment of riches: from Scripture to modern scholarship, we are blessed with a vast and complex theological inheritance. And yet this feast of traditional riches is too frequently inaccessible to the general reader.

The Cascade Companions series addresses the challenge by publishing books that combine academic rigor with broad appeal and readability. They aim to introduce nonspecialist readers to that vital storehouse of authors, documents, themes, histories, arguments, and movements that comprise this heritage with brief yet compelling volumes.

TITLES IN THIS SERIES:

Reading Augustine by Jason Byassee
Conflict, Community, and Honor by John H. Elliott
An Introduction to the Desert Fathers by Jason Byassee
Reading Paul by Michael J. Gorman
Theology and Culture by D. Stephen Long
Creation and Evolution by Tatha Wiley
Theological Interpretation of Scripture by Stephen Fowl
Reading Bonhoeffer by Geffrey B. Kelly
Justpeace Ethics by Jarem Sawatsky
Feminism and Christianity by Caryn D. Griswold
Angels, Worms, and Bogeys by Michelle A. Clifton-Soderstrom
Christianity and Politics by C. C. Pecknold
A Way to Scholasticism by Peter S. Dillard
Theological Theodicy by Daniel Castelo
The Letter to the Hebrews in Social-Scientific Perspective by David A. deSilva
Basil of Caesarea by Andrew Radde-Galwitz
A Guide to St. Symeon the New Theologian by Hannah Hunt
Reading John by Christopher W. Skinner
Forgiveness by Anthony Bash
Jacob Arminius by Rustin Brian
Reading Jeremiah by Jack Lundbom
John Calvin by Donald McKim

APPROACHING JOB

ANDREW ZACK LEWIS

CASCADE *Books* • Eugene, Oregon

APPROACHING JOB

Cascade Companions 33

Copyright © 2017 Andrew Zack Lewis. All rights reserved. Except for brief quotations in critical publications or reviews, no part of this book may be reproduced in any manner without prior written permission from the publisher. Write: Permissions, Wipf and Stock Publishers, 199 W. 8th Ave., Suite 3, Eugene, OR 97401.

Cascade Books
An Imprint of Wipf and Stock Publishers
199 W. 8th Ave., Suite 3
Eugene, OR 97401

www.wipfandstock.com

PAPERBACK ISBN: 978-1-62564-818-1
HARDCOVER ISBN: 978-1-4982-8715-9
EBOOK ISBN: 978-1-5326-1516-0

Cataloguing-in-Publication data:

Names: Lewis, Andrew Zack.

Title: Approaching Job / Andrew Zack Lewis.

Description: Eugene, OR: Cascade Books, 2017 | Series: Cascade Companions 33 | Includes bibliographical references and index.

Identifiers: ISBN 978-1-62564-818-1 (paperback) | ISBN 978-1-4982-8715-9 (hardcover) | ISBN 978-1-5326-1516-0 (ebook).

Subjects: Bible. Job—Criticism, interpretation, etc. | Bible. Job—Theology.

Classification: BS1415.2 L50 2017 (paperback) | BS1415.2 (ebook).

Manufactured in the U.S.A. 03/01/17

Unless otherwise noted, Scripture quotations are from the New Revised Standard Version Bible, copyright © 1989 National Council of the Churches of Christ in the United States of America. Used by permission. All rights reserved worldwide.

For Luke

Now when Job's three friends heard of all these troubles that had come upon him, each of them set out from his home—Eliphaz the Temanite, Bildad the Shuhite, and Zophar the Naamathite. They met together to go and console and comfort him. When they saw him from a distance, they did not recognize him, and they raised their voices and wept aloud; they tore their robes and threw dust in the air upon their heads. They sat with him on the ground seven days and seven nights, and no one spoke a word to him, for they saw that his suffering was very great.

JOB 2:11–13

CONTENTS

Acknowledgments • ix

Introduction • 1

1 Content of the Book of Job • 8

2 Structure and Critical Issues • 44

3 Meaning in Individual Passages • 69

4 Some Theological, Pastoral, and Ethical Implications of the Book of Job • 110

Works Cited • 133
Name Index • 139
Ancient Document Index • 141

ACKNOWLEDGMENTS

I FIRST WANT TO thank Christian Amondson and the whole team at Wipf and Stock for their service. Christian has been a great friend for over a decade now and has encouraged me throughout the process of writing this book. I also greatly appreciate the help from my first reader and another one of my best friends, Dr. Margaret Ramey, who graciously offered comments and encouragement out of the goodness of her heart. I would also like to acknowledge Tom and Ashleen Wartenweiler and the Servants Vancouver Community for inviting me to meals and allowing me to read the book of Job with the community one night a week for two months. Lastly, I could not have completed this manuscript without the support and understanding of my wife, Melanie, and my children, Elaine, Micah, and Luke. Luke was not yet born while I finished up my last book, but was present (napping in the next room) for the composition of the entirety of this one. This book is dedicated to you, Luke: may you remain in awe of Creation and, like Job, seek a face-to-face encounter with the Creator.

INTRODUCTION

Most readers of the book of Job have more in common with Job's friends than with Job himself. Many people have identified with Job over the centuries—whether in their suffering, loss, persecution, or feelings of abandonment. And certainly that is one reason for the perpetual interest in the book. Yet the singular experience of Job as described in the first two chapters—where a wealthy and blessed and perfectly moral man (both the narrator and God describe him as "blameless and upright") suffers the loss of his family, property, and health *because* he is wealthy and blessed and perfectly moral—makes one's ability to identify with Job quite limited. On the other hand, how many of us have found ourselves in comparable situations as Job's friends, particularly as described in 2:11–13? Knowing someone who is suffering and being at a loss as to how to comfort him or her may be an actual universal experience.

Unfortunately, the friends, for the most part, have been vilified for their poor theology based on a moral economy of right for right and wrong for wrong rather than appreciated for their sympathy as they tried comforting their friend in the best way they knew how. Yes, God does condemn their words in 42:7–8. Job's anger at his friends' words along with God's condemnation in the epilogue lead casual readers and scholars alike to dismiss the friends as unsympathetic characters. However, God does offer the friends a route to restoration to the community through Job's intercession in 42:8. Also, only the most dismissive of readers would think that Job's friends argue with Job out of malice rather than with the best of intentions. If most readers are honest with themselves, they can identify with the friends at even their worst—exasperated at the ostensible whining of a friend in a situation the friend could have prevented with a bit more perspicacity. The friends, after all, have no reason to think they should abandon their tradition's retributive theology as they speak into Job's situation.

Very few books have inspired such interest as Job has throughout the centuries, and much of that interest is due to its inscrutability. The work of interpreting Job clarifies the story itself. When the story of Job opens, we meet a blameless, humble man who more than meets God's approval. We don't expect Job to undergo divine testing. As the story unfolds, it shocks us. Just as we think we know what to expect at the start of Job's story, so as interpreters we approach the book familiar with its story or the themes or its theology. Yet as we move closer, the book shocks us again. When confronted with the depth of Job's suffering, Job and his friends try to find meaning in it. Similarly, we interpreters of Job argue over its meaning: either at the minutest level like a single word, or at the meaning of the book as a whole, or even what verses belong in the book at all. These arguments have been going on for centuries.

It is not in the scope of this book to bring an end to these arguments, but rather to highlight them. The purpose of *Approaching Job* is to consider all (or at least the most significant) issues pertinent to the interpretation of the book of Job. In order to explore the book from different angles, I offer four chapters that, like Job's friends, first approach him from a distance and then get closer. I hope such an approach gives readers of Job different ways of reading the book and allows them to identify with the different characters and to understand the variety of Job interpreters across the centuries.

Chapter 1 begins the approach with an overview of the characters and themes. I offer a brief character analysis of each character in the book of Job—from Job and God to Job's friends to Job's children to even the marauders who destroy Job's property. Such an approach is my attempt to give each character his or her due. It is easy either to malign characters for their poor decisions with the benefit of a omniscient narrator or hindsight, or to dismiss them as plot devices. Many readers of Job (and I am thinking of myself here) assume a privileged position. As a white male in North America, I am conditioned to read Job as a book for me. Job the character is a privileged person who loses all of his belongings through no fault of his own. Job is either like me or like others in my peer group. But perhaps Job's understanding of suffering is most akin to my understanding of suffering as a member of a wealthy, male, elite audience.[1] If I see Job as the character most like me in his story, then could taking on the perspectives of other characters open up other ways for me to understand the book of Job? Is Job's wife unfairly marginalized after attempting to persuade Job to curse God and die? The first chapter ends with an overview of some of the themes that arise in the book of Job.

At the end of each section in chapter 1, I raise some questions that come up in the character descriptions within that section. I revisit some of these questions in chapter 2, which offers a more traditional introduction to the book

1. See Clines, "Why Is There a Book of Job?," 1.

of Job—describing the structure of the book, offering evidence for proposing composition date in the Persian era, and detailing the most important critical problems with the book.

Though these critical issues are important, especially for those who will continue to read secondary literature on the book of Job, I do suspect that some readers will have less interest in the issues of this chapter. While I revisit many of these issues in the third chapter, particularly the structures diagrammed, lay readers will be forgiven for skimming the sections on the date and integrity of the book. While formal students will benefit from this information, they will find that the composition date is relatively unimportant for interpreting the book and that I assume a general integrity of the book in the next two chapters, especially in attempting to determine the theology of the book of Job.

The third chapter looks closely at the most important and contentious passages of the book of Job. Through much of this chapter I survey the history of interpretation, including recent research to explore what the book of Job might mean through the lens of a particular passage. Within the long book of Job, several writers and exegetes tend to favor different sections over others, which leads them to argue for competing meanings of the book. Several of these passages that have become so important across the centuries create other problems in interpretation, such as translation. The vast majority of readers of the book of Job read Job in a language other than Hebrew. Even those who know Hebrew, though, will note that the Hebrew of Job is particularly ambiguous in parts, either due to the use of rare words, double entendres, or potentially corrupt texts. This book will not erase these ambiguities, but will highlight them in order to make readers aware of other interpretive possibilities or to

Introduction

challenge presuppositions that blind readers to more nuanced understandings of this already challenging book.

Chapter 4 sums up our exploration of the book of Job with brief overviews of theological and ethical implications of the book. Many people have entered the book of Job because they have suffered greatly, hoping that a biblical book where God answers an innocent sufferer will provide some answers to their own suffering. My final chapter looks at the conclusions of some who have entered the book of Job for such reasons as well as other theological conclusions about the book, having to do, for instance, with the freedom of God and the role of humanity in God's creation.

The fascination with Job over the centuries has been too vast to mention more than a fraction of its receptions in this volume, but even a comprehensive evaluation of the impact of Job would not exhaust its propensity to surprise. No matter how many times we approach the book of Job, even with all of its history in mind, we may, like his friends, still be caught aghast at not having recognized him. Most of my experiences with Job have been in academic contexts, at both Regent College and the University of St. Andrews, as well as through the reading of many books and articles and participating in conference seminars. For the last several years, however, I have been living in what is called the "poorest postal code in Canada"—Vancouver's Downtown Eastside. In preparation for writing this book, I thought it would be worthwhile to read through the book with the people I knew who had more in common with Job than anyone else I knew. The Servants of the Poor community house hosts a daily community meal and Bible study and were gracious enough to let me come to read through the book of Job every Tuesday for about two months a little while ago. Many of the participants suffered from addiction or mental illness. Some were victims of domestic violence or the systemic racism of the state. I was curious how these people might identify with Job, who suffers so much through no fault of his own.

I was surprised on the very first day. Of course I knew that Job came from a place of privilege and that his wealth might strike some of my fellow readers as alien, but some were able to empathize with Job's loss in relevant ways. For instance, in the dark of night, one woman left her abusive husband along with the house whose rent she paid with mostly her own money. She now struggles to pay rent in a city hundreds of miles away from the man she left behind. Another woman lost her mother, sister, and son within a single summer—an experience that served as a riposte to another person who felt that the rapidity of Job's losses seemed almost comic. But one woman did not identify with Job. Rather, she, a woman with severe osteoporosis and speech difficulty, felt a strange affinity toward the Sabeans who, in Job 1:15, make off with Job's oxen and donkeys. Taken aback, I asked her to clarify why she identified with the Sabeans, and she said that whenever she walks through a neighborhood like the British Properties or Shaughnessy—the two most expensive neighborhoods in the area—she is made to feel like a threat to the homeowners staring at her limping along the sidewalks.

One can dismiss such a reading, noting that only a reader's lack of understanding would lead the reader to compare the real threat that marauders posed in the ancient Near East to the benign wandering of a person with physical disabilities in modern Canada. Or perhaps a genre-sensitive rhetorical-critical reading would help this woman understand that the Sabeans are a plot device in a folktale, not a piece of the story to take seriously in a Bible study. However, this woman's reading, though atypical in specifics, exemplifies much of the history of the interpretation of Job. Like many interpreters across the centuries, this woman was drawn into the story through her own personal and unique suffering.

I relate this anecdote to show why people keep returning to the book of Job. Its importance in theology and culture lies partly in its ability to surprise its readers. But it also remains a puzzle to its readers, teaching us something new each time we open it. Another friend of mine, an accomplished theologian who suffers (as some theologians do) from flashes of grandiloquence, claimed to me once that he never truly "understood" the book of Job until he read it through in one sitting. After that reading he claimed to "get its meaning." For some reason, he neglected to tell me its meaning. Perhaps he sensed my suspicion that there exists no possible definitive meaning to such a sprawling book and that anyone who claims to reach a conclusion to the book of Job after one read-through fails to grasp much at all.

What follows, then, is not a commentary, explaining Job, as if such a goal were possible. Rather, as the series title Cascade Companions suggests, this book is meant as a companion, aiding readers of Job through some of the most challenging aspects of the book. I do occasionally offer what I believe are the most fruitful ways of reading through some parts of Job. I hope readers will take my suggestions as possibilities that spur discussion and also spur them back to the text of Job itself—to read it again in a new light.

1

CONTENT OF THE BOOK OF JOB

It is customary in biblical studies to begin a book study by outlining potential historical critical problems with the book. While critical concerns are by no means unimportant for anyone digging deep into Job, most people approach the book with little to no concern for its history of composition or transmission. Most see it, at the very least, as a story with a compelling premise and interesting characters. Many included among such a group (and some outside such a group) approach Job as Scripture, inspired by God and thus authoritative in its received form. This chapter will sketch the book as received in the canon—first with descriptions of the various characters in the book and second outlining various themes of Job.

In many ways, the book of Job reads like a drama. The prose prologue and epilogue offer action fit for the theater,

Content of the Book of Job

where violence is offstage and the important aspects of the story are in the characters' reactions. Two of the most celebrated retellings of Job (Blake's Illustrations of Job and the play *J. B.* by Archibald MacLeish) confirm the dramatic nature of the story. Once the stage is set, so to speak, with the demise of Job's health, wealth, and progeny, the story is told entirely through a dialogue between and among six characters.

The following section, in the spirit of drama, will present the cast of characters in the story.[1] Problems arise when breaking down the story this way. Following the text through the actions of one character raises questions not easy to answer using literary analysis. Scholars in the past couple centuries have been very interested in answering these questions using a variety of tools, namely, text criticism, historical criticism, philosophical theology, and narrative criticism. At the end of each character description will be a question or series of questions to be addressed more in depth in later chapters. Not all questions will have satisfactory answers, but they will rather bring us into the ongoing conversation of Joban scholarship.

THE MAIN PLAYERS

Job

The narrative's description of Job, a Gentile from the East, is of a man who has all the important features of someone wealthy and important during the time of the patriarchs. He had a great deal of livestock (camels, sheep, and oxen) and, presumably, the land on which they could graze. He had many servants to take care of all his belongings and

---

1. I want to be quick to point out, however, that there is no evidence that the book of Job was intended to be performed, only that it shares some similarities with drama.

many children (seven sons and three daughters). Because of this type of wealth, of all the characters of the Bible, he shares the most in common with Jacob/Israel. However, the narrator is careful to point out Job's piety, which separates him from Jacob (and all the other characters of the Bible). The narrator tells us that Job is blameless and upright (*tam weyashar*). This language should remind readers of Yahweh's command to Abram to exhibit these same qualities in exchange for a covenant and many children (Gen 17:1). Job, thus, seems to have fulfilled the covenant Yahweh made with Abram, or a version of it, and he has blessed Job accordingly.

The narrator describes some of Job's actions as concrete evidence of his piety. Job would sacrifice, not only for himself, but especially for his children out of fear that the children may have sinned in their hearts. Later in the story, Job goes into further description of his pious actions. He "delivered the poor who cried, and... was eyes to the blind and feet to the lame." (29:12, 15); he was faithful to his wife (31:9, 10) and clothed the naked (31:19). In short, Job was as perfect as anyone could expect to be and more.

Soon after the narrative establishes Job's stature as the "greatest of all the people of the East" (1:3), Job loses everything in such quick succession that it would be comic if it were not so tragic. Job's story is not true tragedy, however, because he has no tragic flaws. Rather, readers learn that Job loses everything *because* he was blameless and upright. The rest of the story explores the fallout of Job's losses. His initial reaction is a pious response: "Naked I came from my mother's womb, and naked I shall return there; the LORD gave and the LORD has taken away; blessed be the name of the LORD" (1:21). Job, however, is struck by a skin disease, which, along with time to reflect, takes him over the edge to despair. He sits among the ashes in silence (but for a brief

Content of the Book of Job

exchange with his wife) until he initiates a curse against the day of his birth. A long dialogue with his three friends ensues.

One of the questions that arises in the book is whether Job is pious for the sake of piety or whether he does all the right things in expectation of God's blessings. In the words of the Satan character, "Does Job fear God for nothing?" (1:9). This question is difficult to answer, even in retrospect, because it does seem that Job acted as he did with the expectation that he would get something in return. After all, he was righteous and just and was blessed with wealth and children. He should be forgiven for believing so. This belief in what scholars call "retributive theology" would explain why he feels so wronged at times after he does lose everything. He maintains his innocence throughout his dialogues with his friends. If he does not believe in retributive theology, then his innocence would be irrelevant to the discussion. He believes he is wronged by God and begs God for answers. (Job's speeches to his friends all come in two parts: the first part responds directly to his friend, and the second addresses God as the second person.)

A second, related question, which has inspired much debate over the years is, how do the Job of the prologue and the Job of the dialogues relate to each other? In other words, the way Job acts in chapters 1 and 2 seems very different from the way Job acts in the rest of the book. When Job loses everything in chapter 1, he responds with a short hymn of praise. His words allow God to win the wager with the Satan character, which leads to Job being tested again through a skin disease. Even after Job is afflicted with sores all over his body, he asks his wife, "Shall we receive the good at the hand of God, and not receive the bad?" (2:10). Just a few verses later (though seven days later in the narrative), Job explodes, cursing the day of his birth (lit. "his day")

(3:2). There is little in the prologue to prepare readers for this change of attitude. Job sustains his anger throughout the dialogues, revealing little of the meek piety he displays in the prologue.

The difference between the prosaic Job and the poetic Job has been widely noted and discussed for centuries. We will highlight more details of that discussion in the next chapter.

God

The character of God is, likewise, complex. Not allowing the theology of the rest of the canon to influence one's interpretation of God in the book of Job is quite difficult. Nevertheless, it is important to attempt to see who the God of Job is, independent of the rest of the Bible, in order to understand the book of Job. Though readers do encounter God in the prologue, none of the terrestrial characters has any direct interaction with God until chapter 38. In the prologue, God remains in the heavenly court, where the Satan character comes in. God in these first two chapters seems strangely limited in knowledge and power. God asks the Satan where he has come from (1:7) and makes a wager with a created being as if God were unaware of the possible outcomes of such a wager. God even blames the Satan for inciting him "against [Job] to destroy him for no reason" (2:3).

In sharp contrast, when God appears to Job in a tempest in chapter 38, rather than responding to Job's questions and to the justice or injustice of a righteous man suffering, God asks Job a series of rhetorical (even sarcastic) questions on the creation of the world (as opposed to the direct questions God asks the Satan in the prologue). The God of the dialogues is anything but limited. In fact, the entire thrust of the arguments are about God's power and humanity's

Content of the Book of Job

limitations in comparison. Not only does God not ask Job where Job has been as God asks the Satan, but God goes into great and beautiful description of all the things God does know.

Leaving aside the apparent problems between the prosaic God and the poetic God, let us look more closely at the content of God's response to Job. In Job 31:35, Job concludes his final defense of his innocence with a plea. He says, "O that I had one to hear me! (Here is my signature! Let the Almighty answer me!) O that I had the indictment written by my adversary!"[2]

After a speech by the mysterious Elihu, God (going by the proper name Yahweh) eventually responds to Job in 38:2 out of a storm or tempest. The tempest is a destructive force, reminiscent of the great wind that destroys Job's son's house in 1:19, killing all of Job's children. The portrayal of the deity throughout both speeches (chapters 38:1—39:30 and 40:6—41:34) is of a God of power, able to create stars and mountains and willing to unleash creatures uncontrollable by anyone but God. The first part begins with rhetorical questions addressed to Job about the creation of the world and God's continuing control over the elements of the earth and heavens. God reminds Job and readers of the foundation of the earth (38:4–7), the seas (38:8–11), the light and the darkness (38:12–21), the weather (38:22–31), and the stars in the heavens (38:31–33)—all with a sarcasm meant to put Job back in his place. Job's final defense refers to the honor he receives as a wealthy and just lord in

---

2. One would be forgiven for wondering if the word "adversary" is related to the Hebrew word *satan* so that we find Job alluding to the wager in the heavenly court. The word used, however, is the legal term *rîḇ*, more commonly translated "lawsuit," alluding more clearly to a hypothetical court case Job is bringing to God in the dialogues.

his land. God's response shows him how insignificant that honor looks in the grand scheme of things.

God's speech continues (chapter 39) with a litany of wild animals that, unlike Job's livestock, cannot be tamed: lions, ravens, mountain goats, wild donkeys, wild oxen, ostriches, horses, hawks, and eagles. These well-known animals do not require husbandry to survive and thrive; their existence seems mysterious.

God's second speech continues this theme by introducing two new creatures: the Behemoth (40:15–24) and the Leviathan (chapter 41). Much of the speech seems redundant, leading many scholars to conclude that they were added at a later date than the original, but the degree of its superfluity depends in part on how one interprets the meaning of Behemoth and Leviathan. If, as some Bibles suggest in footnotes, the Behemoth is a hippopotamus and the Leviathan is a crocodile, then the passage seems to add little to the argument from the litany of animal creatures in chapter 39. If, however, the Behemoth and Leviathan are mythical creatures, then it adds another dimension to God's response to Job. God is the creator and lord not merely of all one sees, but even of the legendary creatures that may exist only in stories or the imagination and that may represent evil.

The overall message seems to be that God has created and cared for these wildest of the wild animals and the wildest of the wild places. The concerns of humanity are not the only concerns. How this works as a response to Job's suffering, however, is a point of contention. Somehow this satisfies Job, either by intimidating him or through some mysterious epiphany difficult to put into words. Intellectually, however, readers must wonder what is satisfactory about this response to Job's rather specific concerns. There is no mention of the wager or even an acknowledgment of

Content of the Book of Job

Job's innocence (at least not until the epilogue, which is after Job claims to be satisfied).

One thesis, which we will look at again below, is that Yahweh is responding directly to Job's initial speech in chapter 3, where Job wishes he had never been born.[3] Yahweh sees that wish as an assault on the created order and rectifies Job's destructive speech act with his own recreative speech act.

One other aspect to consider before moving on to Job's friends is the name of God in the book of Job. I have mainly been using the generic name "God" throughout this description of the deity. This is how most people likely think of the character described throughout the book of Job. The reality is more complex than this and has also contributed to source-critical discussions on the text. In the prologue, the narrator uses the proper noun of the Israelite god, Yahweh (translated in English Bibles as "the LORD"). Job also uses the Tetragrammaton (the four-letter divine name YHWH, pronounced "Yahweh") in his proverbial response to his losses in 1:21: "The LORD gave, and the LORD has taken away." However, Job calls the deity "Yahweh" only one more time throughout the entire book (12:9). Historical critics may argue that the fact that Yahweh is the preferred name for the deity in the prose section while names derived from the root *ʾel* (such as *ʾel* [54 times], *ʾeloah* [35 times], and *ʾelohim* [3 times], all translated "God" in most English Bibles) predominate in the dialogues between the friends stems from the different sources and traditions that compose the book as a whole. A Yahwist composed the prose folktale while an Elohist composed the poetry. A narrative critic, however, might note that the deity is the same, whether called Yahweh or God, but that Gentile characters

---

3. For a detailed exploration of this thesis, see Alter, *Biblical Poetry*, 96–110.

living in "the east," such as Job and his friends, would not call God by the proper name ascribed to the deity by those living in the Levant, other than in the occasional proverb (i.e. 1:21–22). These are concerns worth considering while reading through the book of Job.

The Narrator

Though not technically a character in the strict sense, the narrator does play an important role in telling the story and in how one might interpret it. For instance, the narrator consistently uses the Tetragrammaton when describing God even though the characters do not (the exception being in 1:1, where the narrator uses the expression "feared God" in describing Job).

Also, like most Old Testament narrators, this narrator describes the events efficiently, without embellishment. Job loses his family and his property in rapid succession and the narrator offers no editorial analysis. The narrator offers no descriptions of the Satan, Yahweh, Job's wife, Job's children or Job's friends other than that which they offer through their own speech. In the dialogues, the narrator merely introduces each new speech with a very brief interruption: literally, "Then Bildad the Shuhite answered, and he said," or "Then Job answered, and he said."

Because of the terseness of the narrator's descriptions of either characters or actions, all the more striking is how much the narrator does describe Job in the opening passage. Job is "blameless and upright," the narrator tells us. "He feared God and turned away from evil." After this description, the narrator sums up Job by describing him as "the greatest of all the people of the east." That the narrator editorializes about Job's character in this way, and that God reiterates the description in 1:8 and 2:3, should be in readers' minds throughout the dialogues. For though the friends and Job speak entirely for themselves from chapters 3 to 31, the readers have insight that the speakers do not. Readers know about the wager, and readers also know the narrator's summation of Job's character, which can be presumed to be authoritative and reliable.

The Friends

The friends (minus Elihu) have been considered three versions of the same person by many, if not most, interpreters in the past. They have also been viewed quite negatively, because Yahweh eventually condemns their words in 42:6, 7. Recently, scholars have been paying them closer attention and judging their words on their own merits.[4] I will try to do the same below, but I will judge the words of each friend separately rather than judging the combined words of all the friends as a group offered by speakers with the same point of view. Each friend has his own name, and they also come from different places—Eliphaz from Teman, Bildad from Shuah, and Zophar from Naamath: so they likely have different personalities, rhetorical styles, and even, perhaps, theologies. If there is something that binds these three characters together, it is a confidence in the depravity of humanity and a general belief in retributive theology. In the context of the story, each of the friends believes that Job must have sinned because all the friends either have consistently seen the wicked punished or have heard that this is the case through tradition (and in Eliphaz's case, through a mystical encounter with a spirit).

---

4. See especially Newsom, *Book of Job*, 90–129.

APPROACHING JOB

Eliphaz the Temanite

Eliphaz speaks first and speaks the most of any of the friends (chapters 4–5, 15, and 22). Despite the shock of Job's first speech, which curses the day of his own birth and seems so utterly hopeless and despairing, Eliphaz's **first speech** is mostly gentle and offers a good starting point for understanding this friend's point of view. Eventually, Eliphaz will become obviously frustrated, and readers will be tempted to think that his emotions are getting in the way of reasoned argument. Nevertheless, whether this happens because Eliphaz is allowed to speak first among the three friends, before Job's intransigence over his own innocence becomes evident, or because of Eliphaz's personality, he comes off as the most even-keeled of the three.

Besides hints of personality, one of the things that distinguish the three friends is their theological method—where they find authority for their positions. Eliphaz offers several examples of his general observations about the world within his speeches, which generally support his thesis that those "who sow trouble reap the same" (4:8b). These observations allow him to conclude that Job's troubles must therefore result in his own behavior, whatever that may be. Readers may note that the syllogism Eliphaz assumes to be true (i.e., those who sow trouble reap trouble; Job has reaped trouble; therefore Job has sown trouble) is flawed, but the flaw appears because Eliphaz has not observed a case such as Job's.

Eliphaz, however, also has another source for his theology that is arguably more authoritative than his own observations. In his first speech, Eliphaz describes a mystical experience he had in which a prophetic word came to him in a nightmare. The experience seems to have been almost like witnessing a poltergeist. The ghost (or perhaps he intends Job to think it is God speaking) asks Eliphaz, "Can mortals be righteous more than God?" (4:17). The scene Eliphaz describes is uncanny and mysterious and open to interpretation. For instance, is the word he receives from a divine source? If so, it would be difficult to argue against it. What we can be more sure about is what Eliphaz's reporting and relying on this mystical vision for guidance says about him, and in particular about his rhetorical strategy. Relaying a secret message to counter Job's first speech allows Eliphaz to support his position not only with his interpretation of his observations but with an outside authority. When Eliphaz's appeal to his spiritual encounter has little effect on Job's demeanor, he abandons the strategy and offers a less gentle retort.

In Eliphaz's **second speech** (chapter 15) there is no mention of any mystical authority, but he does appeal to different outside authority, namely, tradition. Bildad, in chapter 8, has already used tradition to buttress his argument against Job's claims of innocent suffering. Eliphaz's appeal to tradition seems a little different from Bildad's more formal tradition (which we will look at below) in that Eliphaz includes elders' observations alongside his own. Everyone he can think of views the workings of the world in the same way Eliphaz does. He sarcastically asks Job if he was "the first human," anticipating Yahweh's response from the tempest in 38:4–7. More directly, Eliphaz tells Job, "The gray-haired and the aged are on our side, those older than your father" (15:10). Despite his appeals to other people, he still relies mainly on his own observations (sometimes equating lessons from his own experience and the words of others in extended parallelism, as in 15:17, 18), sustaining his main argument from chapter 5: "The wicked writhe in pain all their days."

The general tone of Eliphaz's second speech betrays a loss of patience toward Job. "Should the wise answer with empty knowledge?" he asks. "Should they argue with unprofitable talk?" implying that Job is not wise because he argues with useless words (15:2, 3). In fact, Eliphaz goes further, implying even that Job is wicked (15:20). When Job seems unwilling to concede any of the points of his friends in his following speeches, Eliphaz changes course again (chapter 22).

In his **third speech**, Eliphaz goes from doubting Job's righteousness to wondering why God would even value righteousness. He asks, "Can a mortal be of use to God? . . . Is it any pleasure to the Almighty if you are righteous?" (22:2,3) If readers perceive Eliphaz reaching his wit's end with Job, the evidence continues to mount throughout this short speech. Job is no longer merely not righteous to Eliphaz: he is out-and-out wicked (22:5). In his first speech, Eliphaz grants that Job is righteous enough to have "supported those who have stumbled" (4:4). Job, in the mind of Eliphaz, was marginally pious enough to be confident that God would restore him (4:6). By his third speech, however, the goodwill that Job had for those less fortunate is gone in the memory of Eliphaz. Job has "stripped the naked of their clothing . . . [and has] given no water to the weary to drink . . . [He has] sent widows away empty-handed, and the arms of the orphans [he has] crushed" (22:6–9). After Job mounts his final defense a few chapters later, readers have two competing views of Job.

Because readers are privileged to have a third-person narrator and God's opinion in the prologue, we will find it difficult to side with Eliphaz and his friends concerning Job's piety. However, considering the position in which Eliphaz finds himself—arguing with an increasingly intransigent person whose position, if true, would mean the collapse of his worldview—Eliphaz and his friends likely are a great deal more sympathetic to Job than we often credit them for being.

Bildad the Shuhite

As I stated above, Bildad relies more on the authority of tradition to argue with Job than do either Eliphaz or Zophar. The bulk of his responses are extended proverbs or parables that are not found outside of Job but that give readers the impression that Bildad is repeating wisdom passed down through the generations. Early in his **first speech**, which, like Eliphaz's first speech has a gentleness and encouraging tone that disappear in the later speeches, Bildad suggests that Job "inquire now of bygone generations, and consider what their ancestors have found. For we are but of yesterday, and we know nothing, for our days on earth are but a shadow. Will they not teach you and tell you and utter words out of their understanding?" (8:8-10).

What follows is a parable of two plants that is reminiscent of the tree and chaff in Psalm 1. The godless are like papyrus in a dry marsh, which seem to be healthy but "wither more quickly than grass." The blameless, however, are like a well-watered plant that can be transplanted and flourish elsewhere[5]—the implication being that Job's trials are likely akin to the transplanting of the well-watered plant. Bildad concludes his first speech with the most encouraging line of all the speeches in the book: "He will yet fill your mouth with laughter, and your lips with shouts of joy. Those who

---

5. The parable is notoriously difficult to decipher. The above interpretation has been put forward by several commentators. See especially Newsom, *Book of Job*, 104-5; Gordis, *Book of Job*, 521; Habel, *Book of Job*, 170-78; and Janzen, *Job*, 85-86.

hate you will be clothed with shame, and the tent of the wicked will be no more" (8:21–22).

In his **second speech**, Bildad offers what seems like another lengthy proverb from his tradition. In 18:5, he begins, "Surely the light of the wicked is put out, and the flame of their fire does not shine." The proverb continues with parallel elaboration until the final verse of the speech, which sums up the rest of the speech with "such is the place of one who does not know God."

The differences between the second and first speeches are striking. Bildad's first speech is not merely encouraging; much of what he says is undeniably true. He predicts with remarkable accuracy events that happen at the end of the book. Other than an insensitive swipe at the sins of Job's children in verse 4, it would be very difficult to pinpoint what Bildad says that could be considered "speaking wrong" as God levels at the friends in 42:6,7. Bildad tells Job that if he seeks God and pleads with the Almighty, God will restore Job to his rightful place (8:5,6). This is a far cry from the second speech, where Bildad does not even mention the possibility of restoration for Job. One wonders if he sees no reason to mention the blameless in his proverb since Job clearly does not qualify as blameless in his mind.

If Bildad betrays a frustration in his second speech with the lack of progress he and his friends are making, the **third speech** seems like one from someone who has all but given up in breaking through to his friend. Chapter 25 contains only five verses of speech, very little of which advances the discussion in a way that his previous speeches did. Bildad claims that no one can be pure in God's eyes, not even the stars in the sky, so "how could a human being, who is a worm!" (25:6). As we will see in the next chapter, the final form of the text in the third cycle of speeches contains several thematic and linguistic problems that historical critics have attempted to reconcile by emending the text. One of the factors that has concerned scholars is the brevity of Bildad's third speech. None of the other chapters in the book is nearly as short. However, reading Bildad's speeches back to back to back reveals a different kind of trend: increasing frustration with the dialogue and decreasing patience with Job. Compared to Zophar, however, Bildad is a pillar of patience.

Zophar the Naamathite

Either because he is a naturally less patient or empathic person, or because by the time he gets a chance to speak Job has indicated his unwillingness to listen to the reason of his friends, Zophar enters the dialogue sharply, with very little positive spin on Job's predicament. To be sure, the **first speech** ends with a reason to hope not dissimilar to Bildad's and Eliphaz's, but with an important distinction. Eliphaz recognizes that Job has instructed many (4:3) and that God is merely disciplining Job (5:17). Bildad recognizes the possibility that Job is or could be pure and upright (8:6). Zophar, however, is more direct in his criticism, telling Job to put away the iniquity in his hand. To Zophar, either there is no doubt that Job has sinned, or he does not see the benefit of flattering Job for Job's past righteousness. There is hope in Zophar's first speech, though, for Job could have a brighter future if he only stopped sinning and prayed to God (11:14–21).

In his **second speech**, Zophar, like the others, hints that tradition allows him to make his claim ("Do you not know this from of old, ever since mortals were placed on earth, that the exulting of the wicked is short, and the joy of the godless is but for a moment?" [20:4, 5]), but he is less explicit on where he gets his authority. Zophar has a distinct theology but he does not reveal his sources. His theology seems to be that God punishes the wicked and rewards the righteous, but in the second speech there is no indication that there are righteous people to reward.

The most notable aspect of Zophar's speeches is that there are only two in the final form of the book of Job. For reasons discussed in the next chapter, some scholars have taken it upon themselves to reconstruct Zophar's **third speech** from some of Job's words in chapter 27 while others have found reason to maintain the final form of the book (1) because there are no extant versions of the reconstructed text or any indication from early sources that there were any scribal errors in the third cycle of speeches, and (2) because Zophar's earlier speeches may reveal a personality that becomes so frustrated with Job's recalcitrance that he finds it futile to speak at all.

Elihu the Buzite

Elihu the Buzite is in equal parts the most controversial character in the book of Job and, ironically, the most ignored. Some critics all but dismiss him because all of the other characters in the story ignore him too. These critics feel that if no characters mention Elihu, then that is likely due to a later writer inserting Elihu's speeches into an already existing text. That is, Job and his friends do not mention Elihu being present through any of the dialogues, and Yahweh does not praise him or condemn him as he does the other four participants because Elihu is not actually present for the story. Other readers, however, have taken the ignorance of the other characters about Elihu as a sign that he is to be taken *more* seriously than the others. For if Yahweh rebukes Job in 38:2 and 40:2 and condemns the speeches of Eliphaz and his "two friends" in 42:7, 8 but says nothing

Content of the Book of Job

of Elihu, then we must determine that Yahweh tacitly approves of Elihu's speeches.

We will look more closely at the critical issues regarding the text of Elihu and the rest of the book of Job in the next chapter. Here, we recognize Elihu as a character in the book of Job for the simple reason that we have no ancient versions of the book of Job that exclude Elihu. In short, Elihu is no less a canonical or canonized figure than Job, so we must at least give him the benefit of the doubt, even if we eventually determine that Yahweh in the book of Job did not rebuke him because Yahweh did not, at the time of speaking, know of his existence in the narrative.

What we can say about Elihu, based on the final form of the book of Job, is that he is the youngest of the speakers in the dialogues and that he has the only Hebrew name among Job and his three friends. His father, Barachel, also has a Hebrew name, and one that is relatively common among minor characters in the Hebrew Bible (cf. 1 Sam 1:1; 1 Chr 12:20; 26:7; and 27:18). Barachel, however, is a Buzite, which is not a known Israelite or Judahite tribe, but is likely Arabian, like the other of Job's friends.[6] Elihu's long introduction, compared with those of his friends, is curious and has been sited as evidence of a later entry into the book.

When he finally does speak, Elihu spends quite a bit of space introducing his own speech, even after the narrator spends five verses explaining who Elihu is and why he has not spoken yet. He explains himself that he is young and therefore timid to speak up. But he is frustrated with Job's friends' arguments and so feels obligated to add his two cents. After the lengthy two-part introduction, much of what Elihu says resembles the words of Job's other friends. The similarity between what Job's other friends say and what Elihu says also contributed to Elihu's being ignored

6. Pope, *Job*, 242.

by readers. By the time one reaches chapter 32, readers are ready for the climax, and so Elihu seems like a chore to include in one's reception of the dialogue.

There are differences between Elihu and the others, however, though these differences may seem subtle to us. Elihu claims to receive his authority not from his own experience or wisdom as the others do, but from God. Whereas Eliphaz receives word from an unnamed spirit (4:12–16), Elihu has no doubt that "his maker" (*pōʿălî*) has given him this information. "For truly my words are not false," he boasts, "one who is perfect in knowledge is with you" (36:4). The effect on readers can be one of three: readers can brush Elihu aside as no different from the other friends, who have equally flawed personalities that move them to speak wrongly;[7] the reader can view Elihu's author as a later reader of Job who has inserted a new point of view from a later era;[8] or the reader can take Elihu at his word, viewing him as a first-stage response to Job and his friends.[9] In this last view, Elihu's name is a partial key to understanding him as a intermediary for God. Like Daniel and Ezekiel, Elihu belongs to the tradition of prophets who speak through dreams and visions.[10] And indeed, Elihu offers several other examples of these types of inspiration (32:18; 33:4, 23). Elihu also anticipates some of what Yahweh says about weather in the following speeches, spending much of chapters 36–37 describing a winter storm.

Another of these subtle differences can be found in chapter 33, where Elihu encourages Job to repent of his sins. Though repentance seems like a theme that Eliphaz and the others touch on, there are subtle differences between what

7. Longman, *Job*, 400.
8. Newsom, *Book of Job*, 200–205.
9. Seow, *Job 1–21*, 31–37.
10. Ibid., 34.

the friends say and what Elihu says. The friends suggest that Job will escape his troubles and may even prosper, but not through repentance per se. Rather, either Job will be chastened by God's correction (5:17), or Job could reverse the punishment by being pure and upright (8:6); but more often, Job will simply be restored in due time. Elihu, on the other hand, encourages Job to admit he has sinned, not because he is arrogant as the friends seem to imply, but as a method of repentance and restoration (33:23–28). Thus Elihu distinguishes himself from the friends and may even anticipate Job's responses to Yahweh's speeches in 40:4–5 and 42:2–6.

THE MINOR CHARACTERS

hassatan[11]/Satan

Most English translations of the book of Job use the proper noun "Satan" when labeling this mysterious character, which can be quite misleading due to the centuries of development the character of the fallen angel called Satan has undergone since the writing of the book of Job. In fact, there is no real reason to identify these two characters in religious history—the Satan in Job and the fallen angel later known as the devil—with each other. Yet it is true that the character found in the first two chapters of Job has been used to develop our understanding of the devil.

The problem with identifying *hassatan* in the book of Job with, say, Satan from *Paradise Lost*, stems partly from the way the Hebrew word *satan* is used in Job and elsewhere

---

11. The proper spelling of this word using diacritical marks is *haśśāṭān*. I have taken the diacritical marks out of this word for the sake of simplicity.

in the Hebrew Bible. Consider that the *ha* in *hassatan* is the definite article, making the *satan* unlikely to be a proper noun. In fact, *hassatan* is not the only angelic character in the Bible to be described with that noun. In Num 22:22, the angel of the LORD, who represents Yahweh on earth, "took his stand in the road as [Balaam's] *satan*." In the case of Num 22, a *satan* is a character who opposes someone else. (English versions translate it as "adversary.") In the book of Zechariah (which appears to be from the same historical time period as the book of Job), verses 1 and 2 of chapter 3 feature the same name for a character similar to the one in Job: *hassatan* stands to the right of Yahweh to accuse (lit. "to *satan*") the high priest Joshua. *Hassatan*, therefore, seems to be a special office that a particular celestial being assumes. Many commentators on Job, therefore, describe *hassatan* as something akin to a modern district attorney, who prosecutes cases for the sake of the justice system, rather than as a purely diabolical character set to destroy God's plan.[12] This may help explain why *hassatan* seems tethered in some ways to the commands of Yahweh—he offers suggestions about how to test Job's piety but cannot go further in testing him than God will let him.

The way *hassatan* goes about his testing is unclear in the first part of the wager. In 1:12, after Yahweh grants him permission to test his theory of Job's interested piety, *hassatan* departs from Yahweh's presence, and the point of view shifts to that of the earthbound beings. "One day," the narrator says, terrible things happen to Job in quick succession, and there is no indication that the terrestrial characters

---

12. Though *hassatan* is not to be seen as identical to the Satan of Dante or modern Protestantism, there is a sense that he does not have pure motives, either. In Zech 3:1–2, *hassatan* appears opposite the Angel of the Lord and accuses Joshua the high priest. Yahweh rebukes *hassatan* in order to defend Joshua, in much the same way Yahweh does for Job in opposition to *hassatan* in Job 1–2.

Content of the Book of Job

recognize that *hassatan* has anything to do with them (or that *hassatan* is even exists). In fact, one of Job's servants describes one event as "fire of God" falling from the sky. The servant's description foreshadows all the other characters' assessments of what befalls Job: God is the instigator of Job's woes, not Satan, *hassatan*, or any other diabolical figure. That being said, *hassatan* is more directly involved in Job's physical suffering. It is *hassatan* who afflicts Job with painful sores in 2:7. However, again, the terrestrial beings only suspect God to be the perpetrator of the sores, for Job's wife suggests that Job curse God and die (2:9). Also, though Job disagrees with his wife as to how to respond to his suffering, he agrees that God is the one from whom he is accepting both good and trouble (2:10).

From the perspective of the rest of the book of Job, *hassatan* acts mainly as a plot device. Job is a pious and blessed man, and everything would theoretically continue as is without some sort of conflict. Thus, a mysterious figure proposes a challenge to God that eventually sets the real narrative (a theological dialogue between Job and his friends and God) in motion. The Satan-as-prop thesis is corroborated by the fact that *hassatan* disappears after Job 2:7 and is never mentioned again, even in the epilogue. Job never even finds out about *hassatan*. Though there is some truth to that view of *hassatan*, he asks an important question that resonates throughout the dialogues even though he is not present to find out how it is answered. He asks Yahweh, "Does Job fear God for nothing?" (1:9) Much of the rest of the book of Job seeks to answer this question, for when Job does lose everything as part of the wager between *hassatan* and Yahweh, readers wait to see how Job will respond now that he has no evidence of blessing from God. The friends play with the question unknowingly, by suggesting that because Job is suffering, he must not have feared God after all or been as pious as he seemed.

There are potentially other allusions to *hassatan* and his question throughout the rest of the book. In Job 9:17, Job turns *hassatan*'s question on its head, saying that God crushes him with a tempest (foreshadowing the tempest in which God will appear in chapter 38) and "multiplies [his] wounds without cause" (repeating the same word [*chinnam*] *hassatan* uses in 1:9, which the NRSV translates "for nothing"). From Job's perspective, the disinterested party is God, who has ignored Job's piety and attacked him for no reason.

Job's Wife

Job's wife has a surprisingly small role in the book of Job, considering how much she lost along with Job. She is only mentioned explicitly three times in the book (2:9; 19:17; and 31:10) and says only one thing: "Do you still persist in your integrity? Curse God and die." (2:9) Like *hassatan*, she is merely a plot device meant to show how serious Job's situation is and how pious he remains in that situation. Job's wife does not understand how Job could not curse God because of his suffering. In fact, she is encouraging Job to do exactly what *hassatan* predicted he would do after his "bones and flesh" are stricken in 2:5, which brings up the possibility that the "bones and flesh" is a double entendre, for the word not only refers to Job's literal bones and flesh but is a common metonymy for "family" in the Hebrew Bible (cf. Gen 2:23; 29:14; Judg 9:2; 2 Sam 5:1; etc.)[13] If *hassatan* "touched" Job's wife, that would explain why she encouraged Job to

---

13. See Seow, *Job 1–21*, 303, who suggests that the bones and flesh may refer to Job's children, which would not make sense since they have already been "touched" in chapter 1.

curse God and also would mean that Job's resistance to her suggestion in 2:10 would prove God's own part in the wager was right.

It is important to note here that Job's wife does not literally encourage Job to "curse God" but rather to "bless God." Almost all English translations take her words as euphemistic, but there have been some translations, the Targum included, that have maintained the literal meaning. This raises the possibility that the offense in Job's wife's statement was not that Job curse God but that he die. It would also add a wrinkle to Job's first speech, in which he curses the day of his birth, indicating a desire to die. Does he, then, reconsider his wife's suggestion upon a week's reflection despite calling her an "outrageous" woman in 1:10? Most likely the narrator uses the euphemism "bless" to mean "curse," since the euphemism is used consistently throughout the first two chapters when it seems most likely to mean "curse" (1:5; 1:11; 2:5).

The other mentions of Job's wife are likewise not flattering to a woman who married the "greatest of all the people of the East." First, grieving his current state, Job claims in 19:17 that his wife finds his breath offensive. Second, he includes her in an oath in 31:10—namely he swears that if he has lusted after another woman, then may his wife sleep with other men. Most curiously to our modern eyes is the narrator's omission of her in the epilogue. When Job receives everything back double and even begets ten more children as a blessing from Yahweh, there is no mention of the woman who gave birth to the children. Job's wife's omission is a reminder of both her status in the story as a plot device and, perhaps, of a wife's status in ancient southwest Asia.

Job's Children

Further evidence that the story is Job's and no one else's comes from the treatment of Job's children. Even the male children, who are grown and likely have full social status in the culture, exist mainly as objects of the narrative. The size of Job's family gives the impression upon which *hassatan* elaborates: God has blessed Job because of his piety. The number of Job's children, seven sons and three daughters, adds to his importance—seven and three being numbers that represent wholeness in Israel. Despite their being a sign of Job's blessing, his children also seem to be a source of his fear of calamity. The sons' wealth allows them regular feasts (the Hebrew is unclear whether they would have seven feasts in a year on their respective birthdays or a feast every day of the week), and Job would find it necessary for him to make sacrifices afterward on their behalf just in case they "cursed God in their hearts." (1:4, 5) It is during one of these feasts that Job loses everything, including his ten children. Job does not seem at all convinced that his children are at fault. However, Bildad seems to think their deaths resulted from their own sins (8:4). Readers know, however, that their deaths are a result of the wager between *hassatan* and Yahweh.

Despite the absence of Job's wife in the epilogue, as mentioned above, Job does beget the same number of children again after God's speech from the tempest. (42:13) The narrator seems unconcerned that the children could not possibly replace the ones lost, however much joy they would bring Job in his old age. Also, despite patriarchy inherent in Job's story (revealed by the choice to center on Job himself, the lone surviving male involved in his tragedy), the last few verses of the book suggest a progressiveness rare in ancient texts—for only Job's daughters are given names among his second set of children. Not only that, but the narrator specifies that they were the most beautiful in all the land and, more important, that Job gave them an inheritance along with their brothers.

Job's Servants

Like all of the minor characters, Job's servants act mainly as plot devices—a mark of Job's wealth in one case and a way to deliver the news of Job's loss of property without Job having to be present at it. The only servants who appear in the text are described as messengers, and there is some ambiguity regarding them. For instance, in 1:15, 16, 17, and 19, the word *na'ar* is used to describe what most translations render "servants" in 15, 16, and 17, and "young people" in 19. In verse 19, the antecedent for "young people" is Job's children. But in each of these verses, the messenger, *mal'ak*, declares that he is the only one to have escaped. The most likely interpretation of these events is that Job's servants, who are all young men, die at the hands of the Sabeans in 15, the fire of God in 16, and the Chaldeans in 17 while taking care of the livestock, and that other servants are serving Job's children at their party when the wind knocks down their house killing all but one inside. One must not think too hard about other interpretations due to the almost tragic-comical nature of the scene, where Job loses all of his belongings to both human activity in 15 and 17 and to what insurance companies today would call "acts of God" in 16 and 19. The messengers/servants, again, are plot devices meant to lead readers to the existential debate in the dialogues. Job, in fact, does not even mention his servants in his final defense.

Sabeans and Chaldeans

There is some confusion over the identity of these two names. (*Sabean* is the name of groups of people from modern-day Yemen, East Africa, and the oasis of Tema in Arabia; *Chaldean* is the name for marauders in both Babylonia and at the same oasis of Tema where the Sabean group could be found.) But most believe that both peoples most likely come from the northern Arabian oasis of Tema. (Job refers to both Tema and Sheba [the same root as in 1:15] in 6:19. These peoples may have even been enemies. Like several of the above characters, these two people groups serve mainly as plot devices, destroying part of Job's property at the command of *hassatan*. However, they do raise interesting questions about the role of other people in the determination of Job's fate. The wager in heaven makes it clear that Job suffers at the hands of *hassatan* and with the approval of Yahweh, but the mechanics of Job's losses are not specified. One can imagine the ability of celestial beings to use the "fire of God" and a "mighty wind" to destroy property, but how does an angel inspire a caravan of marauders? The question goes unanswered and is relatively unimportant in the grand scheme of the book of Job. Yet this is a theological question that many people have asked.

THEMES

As the characters profiled above interact, different themes percolate through the dialogues. Though there are, no doubt, others that could be discussed, the following themes—trial imagery, prayer, wisdom, suffering, and creation—are the most pervasive and important to the book of Job.

The Trial

The theme of the trial is important enough to the book of Job that several Job-inspired creative works focus almost exclusively on the trial aspect of the book when retelling the story.[14] Most commentators agree that the legal language begins in earnest in chapter 9, where Job questions how mortals can prove their innocence to God (9:2), perhaps following that up by bringing a suit against God. The suit reflects a desire to argue with God face to face so that Job can begin to understand what he has done to deserve his fate. Job peppers this speech with forensic vocabulary, such as words concerning innocence and guilt, adversaries, testify, justice, judges, and disputes.[15] However, forensic imagery appears earlier in the dialogues, such as when Eliphaz describes the fool's children being crushed at the "gate" [*šaʿar*], which is where legal issues are decided (e.g., Deut 25:7; Isa 29:21). Even in the prologue, though, one sees *hassatan* acting not like a demon but rather like a district attorney, arguing cases before the high court (1:6–12; 2:1–6). Thus, though some might see Job bringing a suit to God in chapter 9 (with few expectations of success, one might add), the narrative has foreshadowed the trial.

Once the trial begins, Job, the friends, and Elihu sustain it until Yahweh visits Job from the tempest. Job says to God, "Do not condemn me" in 10:2; in 13:6–8, he accuses his friends of arguing God's case for God; he alludes to a witness that will advocate for him in 16:19. In chapter 23, Job continues pleading his case, and he offers his final defense, not just for his innocence, but also his exemplary character, in 29–31.

---

14. Two are aptly named *The Trial of God* by Elie Wiesel and *The Trial* by Franz Kafka.

15. See Seow, *Job 1–21*, 541–42.

Most important in the history of interpretation, Job declares in 19:25, "I know that my redeemer lives"—"redeemer" [*gōēl*] being a legal term referring to one's nearest relative who bears responsibility for someone in legal disputes.[16] Who is Job's redeemer? That is almost impossible to determine with any confidence. The ubiquity of George Frideric Handel's *Messiah* has made it very difficult for people not to associate the redeemer with Christ, though the Old Testament context obviously complicates that hypothesis. Many have argued that God alone could be the redeemer, and the rest of the passage (up to verse 29), where Job warns his friends of their own impending judgment supports that thesis. Others have offered different possible redeemers, such as other deities or other unnamed humans, with little agreement among scholars.[17] Though the meaning of the passage in the context of Job has led to no consensus, that lack of consensus on the meaning of the text does not lessen the text's profundity. Indeed, the whole idea of putting God on trial is so profound that the motif persists in modern literature as one of the main ways Job has inspired people today.

The motif of the trial is, as one scholar puts it, "a medium of exploration, by which Job can configure and reconfigure his situation."[18] A trial allows Job to distance himself from his emotional reaction to his losses and perceived guilt and to call for some objectivity. The only problem for Job is that the one he is bringing to court also happens to be the judge and may even be his lead witness. Nevertheless, Job persists until God responds and satisfies him with the trial, no matter the results.

---

16. See Deut 19:6–12; Ruth 3:9–12, etc.

17. Seow (*Job 1–21*, 823) offers a fairly current list of these variant hypotheses.

18. Newsom, *Book of Job*, 154.

Content of the Book of Job

Creation

When Yahweh finally responds to Job's call for a trial, the response seems irrelevant at first. As I discussed above, the voice from the whirlwind does not seem to answer Job's complaints directly. Rather, Yahweh offers a magnificent retelling of the creation narrative, highlighted with biting sarcasm: "Where were you when I laid the foundation of the earth? Tell me if you have understanding?" (38:4) How does this answer Job's questions? It does not. Rather, according to Robert Alter, it is a direct response to Job's first speech in chapter 3, where Job curses the day of his birth.[19] Much of what Job had wished for in chapter 3, namely, darkness on the day of his birth, Yahweh refutes. Job asks God not to care about the day, but throughout the four chapters from the tempest, we learn that God does care for all of creation, even those things that seem least important to humanity. For Job, the Leviathan is merely a tool used to wreak destruction on a day of Job's concern (3:8). For Yahweh, the Leviathan is something only God can control, and whose purpose shall remain a mystery to humanity (41:1–34). Creation, we learn from the tempest, is not something for humanity to control (as has been implied in some readings from Gen 1:28). Job cannot call for the destruction of a day and think that should be okay. Job's suffering is something that Yahweh will deal with in due time, but not before creation is restored by divine fiat. As we will see in the following chapter, one reading of the structure of the book of Job places Job's first speech in a chiastic relationship with the speeches from the tempest.

Elihu, as discussed above, anticipates the creation-focused speech from the tempest throughout the last chapter of his own speech where he describes a winter storm that

19. Alter, *Biblical Poetry*, 96–110.

only God can control. Otherwise, the theme of creation is mainly relegated to Job's first speech and Yaheweh's last two speeches.

However, there is also evidence that the narrator had the creation narratives of Genesis in mind throughout the prologue.[20] We will see that the narrator alludes to Abraham when describing Job in the next chapter. But Job also shares attributes with Adam from the garden of Eden. One could argue that the characters in the prologue are analogous to the characters in the garden of Eden: Job is Adam, a unique figure without sin who is tested; Yahweh is Yahweh God, an authoritative deity who allows for the possibility of calamity; *Hassatan* is the serpent, a diabolical figure eager to test the limits of the human characters' virtues; and Job's wife is Eve, encouraging Job to sin by cursing God and dying (where dying is the penalty for transgressing Yahweh God's law in the garden [Gen 2:17]). The events of Job also take place in "the East," which is where Eden lies.

Wisdom

The existence of creation language in the book of Job should be no surprise given that the book participates in the genre called wisdom literature. One of the defining features of wisdom literature is an interest in creation. As we have seen in the speech from the tempest, Hebrew creation narratives are not confined to Genesis. And, in fact, we find creation narratives in many passages in the Hebrew Bible deemed wisdom literature. Prov 8:22–36 imagines the personification of Wisdom present at the foundation of the world, and a deuterocanonical work, Sirach 42:15—43:33, discusses the marvels of nature and how God has created and sustained them. Much of Ecclesiastes and Proverbs also

20. Meier, "Job I–II," 183–93.

Content of the Book of Job

meditate on the natural world as Job and his friends do in their dialogues (e.g., Bildad in 8:11–19).

Others have noted common themes throughout wisdom literature found also in Job, such as the significance of a personal name, the difficulty of life, and the problem of retribution.[21] Beyond common themes associated with wisdom literature, the book of Job also shares with other writings the theme of wisdom itself—in particular, the so-called hymn to wisdom in chapter 28. The hymn has caused quite a bit of consternation, some of which we will look at in the next chapter. The main issue is that the hymn's speaker seems undefined. Though the poetry is not dissimilar to the rest of the dialogues between Job and his three friends, it is unclear who of them would be speaking it. Though the lack of a heading makes Job the most likely candidate (as a continuation of the speech Job gives in chapter 27), the already considerable critical issues of chapter 27 throw such a hypothesis into question. Also, the assured theme of the poem itself, that the wisdom for which Job has been begging since chapter 3 is all but impossible to attain outside of piety, is incongruous with the protestations of a man who remains oblivious to the origins of his suffering.

After a beautiful but lengthy description of the hiddenness of wisdom—its being like precious stones deep in the earth to be mined—the poet (perhaps the narrator editorializing and foreshadowing the speech from the tempest) claims that God understands how to find wisdom. In fact, as creator of the earth, God provides access to wisdom. The final phrase—"Truly, the fear of the Lord, that is wisdom; / and to depart from evil is understanding"—presumably from the mouth of God, not only works as a conclusion to the poem but posits a wrinkle in the narrative that serves to foreshadow (with some irony) the thesis of the book of Job.

21. See Murphy, *Tree of Life*, 33–34.

Job, after all, has been arguing for answers to his suffering from God alone, and here we receive some wisdom from God, which is essentially that Job has already accessed wisdom without knowing it. If "the fear of the Lord" is wisdom and "to depart from evil" is understanding (a parallel term to *wisdom*), then Job is already wise, for in the very first verse of the book of Job, the narrator introduces readers to the main character by telling us that Job has indeed "feared God" and "departed from evil."

Prayer

Carol Newsom, while describing the friends' arguments, makes a keen observation about their urging Job to "engage in the practice of prayer."[22] She writes that "the friends are directing him to an important resource of power that he may appropriate for himself, and by doing so gain some control over his experience of turmoil."[23] Prayer, from the viewpoint of Job's friends, is a physical activity, where the suppliant orients oneself toward God (5:8; 8:5), "stretch[es] out [one's] hands toward him" (11:13); distances sin from oneself (11:14); and lifts his or her face to God (11:15). The suppliant is then ready to receive instruction from God and "lay up ... words in [one's] heart" (22:22). Thus, prayer is a tool, indeed a physical tool, Job can use to regain favor from God and restore his life.

There is an irony regarding the friends' call for prayer. After the sustained call from the friends (in chapters 5, 8, 11, and 22) Job in fact does pray, in 42:8–10, but he does not pray for his own salvation. Rather, he prays for his friends—those who instructed Job to pray for himself. When Job prays for them, Yahweh accepts his prayer (42:9) and makes

22. Newsom, *Book of Job*, 109–15.
23. Ibid., 109.

him prosperous again. So a simple reading seems to suggest that Job's prayers for his friends may have saved his friends and resulted in his own prosperity. However, as we will look at a little more closely in the following chapter on structure, Job's prayers for his friends mirror his sacrificing for his children in 1:5. Though the narrator does not explicitly say that Job "prayed" for his children, the similarities between the two passages—one after the narrator explains the extent of Job's wealth and blessings, and the other just preceding the restoration of his wealth and blessings—along with the association of prayer with physical action lead readers to assume that prayer is likely a part of the sacrificial ritual in the first chapter as much as it is explicitly in the final chapter.

Another irony about the friends' call for Job to pray is that Job does pray to God consistently throughout the dialogues, which are bookended by the prayers in 1:5 and 42:8. In 16:17, Job explains to Eliphaz that he has prayed and his prayer is pure, but his hope for a good response from God to that prayer wanes by 24:12, where he declares that God does not hear the cries of those dying in the city. Nevertheless, Job prays consistently throughout the book, even if readers cannot see the rituals that the friends are calling Job to practice. In every single speech that Job gives in response to his friends, Job shifts from talking about God in the third person to talking to God in the second person (usually marked by the editors with the change from one chapter to the next in Job's two-chapter speeches). Job's friends, however, never pray themselves. One interpretation of 42:7–8 is that when Yahweh condemns the friends while praising Job, he tells Eliphaz, Bildad, and Zophar that they have not "spoken rightly *to* me as my servant Job has."[24] In fact, "you did not speak rightly to me" would be the literal translation

24. E.g., Fokkelman, *Book of Job in Form*, 318 (italics added).

of *lōʾ dibbartem ʾēlay nəkônāh*, and seems to be how Jerome read the passage according to his Latin translation.[25] However one translates God's final decision about Job (the majority of translators gloss the prepositional phrase *ʾēlay* as "about me"), Job certainly is the only one of his group to pray to God as long as we understand prayer to be, at minimum, speech directed towards the deity.

Suffering

Of course there is also the question of suffering, which pervades the book and indeed is the impetus for the dialogues. Job, a wealthy man with a large family and good health, loses all his belongings, including his family, and suffers great pain to boot. Interestingly, the dialogues rarely refer back to the details of the prologue. There are exceptions, but even they are vague. For instance, Bildad mentions that Job's children suffered a penalty commensurate with their sin but does not indicate even that they died. Later, in Job's final defense, Job offers details about his life previous to the heavenly wager, but these are not at all identical to those of the prologue (though the honor he receives from the townsfolk [29:7–25] would be expected of the man described in 1:1–3).

Importantly, the lack of specificity or historical data in the dialogues has allowed people to identify more freely with Job, imagining their own suffering and deservedness thereof being litigated by the characters in the book. (Perhaps the generalness is one of the many reasons for the enduring interest in Job from philosophers, artists, and theologians.) In the introduction, I mentioned a reading group I led on the book of Job in Vancouver's poorest neighborhood. One week while discussing one of Job's speeches,

25. *non estis locuti coram me rectum.*

a woman was brought to tears because Job's words told her that she was not alone in her suffering. She, of course, had not lost all that Job had lost, because she had never had much to begin with, but her suffering was likely no less than Job's. Therefore it was not the details or historicity of Job's life that spoke to her but the reality of his emotions that gave her some comfort.

We will return to the theme of suffering in the fourth chapter. The question of suffering is directly related to the question of theodicy, which is not a theme so much as a common interpretation for the book of Job. The fourth chapter will look more closely at different strategies of interpreting Job along with themes that are less literary than theological, among which theodicy predominates in the history of the interpretation.

Before exploring the meaning of Job, though, we need to explore more what this book of Job is. Throughout this chapter on characters and themes, questions of consistency in the text have arisen, and these, along with the structure of the book, are the topics of the next chapter.

REVIEW QUESTIONS

1. How do the Job of the prologue (chapters 1–2) and the Job of the dialogues (Job 3–31) relate to one another?

2. Compare and contrast the God of the prologue (Job 1–2) to the God of the speeches from the tempest (Job 38–41).

3. How do Job's friends differ from one another? Compare and contrast their theologies, theological methods, and rhetorical styles.

4. What do the characters of *hassatan* and Job's wife contribute to the story of Job?

2

STRUCTURE AND CRITICAL ISSUES

STRUCTURE

BIBLICAL BOOKS TEND TO be very carefully structured, and the book of Job is certainly no exception. Any cursory reading of the book will reveal a basic plot, highlighted in part by transition from the prose prologue to the poetic dialogues and back to the prose epilogue. While the prologue and epilogue are highly stylized, chapters 3–41 are almost entirely in parallel couplets, where the second line correlates to the first in some way. Such parallelism marks ancient Semitic poetry and distinguishes it from prose.[1]

---

1. It bears mentioning that such distinctions between prose and poetry remain controversial among biblical scholars. The matrix upon which poetry and prose stand is often viewed as a continuum. Being that as it may, the prologue and epilogue are clearly much closer to the prose side of the continuum, while the dialogues are on the far end of the poetry side.

Structure and Critical Issues

As we will see, the tidiness of the structure has been the basis for historical-critical speculation, especially in those passages that do not conform to our understanding of tidiness. However, we have no versions of Job that differ from those offered in our modern translations, so the following section will present only structures allowed by our extant text. More importantly, the structure's utility is not limited to only historical-critical concerns but can also aid in interpretation. The following two proposed structures for the book of Job do just that.

The first detailed structure follows the chapters of the book first laid out in the late Middle Ages and still used today. Following these chapters, one can then place each into larger groups. The first two chapters make up the prologue, introducing Job's ordeal. The third chapter, Job's monologue after his losses, introduces the dialogues, which can be divided into four sections—dialogues with friends, Job's final defense, Elihu's speeches, and Yahweh's speeches. The final section (chapter 42) is the narrative epilogue.

Each of these broad sections can be delineated into smaller groups: The first two chapters have different scenes—four in the earthly town of Uz and two in the celestial courts. The dialogues with the friends are divided into three cycles, where each friend gives a speech, followed by Job's response. In the third cycle, however, Zophar does not speak. Job offers a final defense after the three speeches. Included in the final defense is a hymn to Wisdom, which may or may not be from the mouth of Job. If Job does not speak the hymn to Wisdom, we are given no other possibilities other than the narrator himself. After Job's final defense, Elihu speaks for five chapters. Yahweh has the final word in the dialogues, taking four chapters and concluding with his verdict in the first part of the epilogue. The final few verses narrate Job's restoration back to a similar state as that of before Job's losses.

Basic Structure of the Book of Job

I. Prologue (chapters 1–2)
    A. First Test (1)
    B. Second Test (2)

II. Dialogues with Friends (chapters 3–41)
    A. Job Curses "His Day" (3)
    B. First Cycle of Speeches (4–14)
        1. Eliphaz (4–5)
        2. Job (6–7)
        3. Bildad (8)
        4. Job (9–10)
        5. Zophar (11)
        6. Job (12–14)
    C. Second Cycle of Speeches (15–21)
        1. Eliphaz (15)
        2. Job (16–17)
        3. Bildad (18)
        4. Job (19)
        5. Zophar (20)
        6. Job (21)
    D. Third Cycle of Speeches (22–27)
        1. Elphaz (22)
        2. Job (23–24)
        3. Bildad (25)
        4. Job (26–27)
    E. Job's Final Defense (28–31)
        1. Hymn to Wisdom (28)
        2. Final Defense (29–31)

III. Elihu (chapters 32–37)

IV. Yahweh's Speeches (chapters 38–41)

V. Epilogue (chapter 42)
    A. Job's Response to Yahweh (42:1–6)
    B. Yahweh's Verdict (42:7–9)
    C. Job's Restoration (42:10–17)

One can see here the flow of the plot from the three cycles of dialogues with the friends, Elihu's interruption and Yahweh's climactic theophany from the tempest. Yahweh gets the final word, and the epilogue brings the narrative to a close. This structure also highlights the fact that Zophar does not have a speech in the third cycle and that Eliphaz's speeches get shorter after the first cycle. The third cycle also contains a very brief speech from Bildad. Below we will encounter some historical-critical theories as to the reasons for such a brief third cycle, but narrative-critical exegetes can also couple what the structure highlights with the progressively turbulent comments offered by the friends throughout the three cycles, concluding that Bildad is losing his patience to the point of saying very little, and that Zophar has given up arguing with Job altogether.

In addition to the above, rather standard structure, one can also determine other structures based on themes. The outline below arranges the book of Job chiastically, where themes or events from the first half of the text are repeated in the second half of the text in reverse order. A chiasm, a common method of organization in the Hebrew Bible and other texts of ancient Southwest Asia, can appear at the macro and micro levels, both thematically and grammatically. For an example of a grammatical *and* thematic chiasm that occurs in a single verse, look at Job 4:12 below, where the NRSV has Eliphaz say, "Now a word came stealing to me, / my ear received the whisper of it." The BHS,[2]

---

2. An acronym of *Biblia Hebraica Stuttgartensia*, the most commonly used Hebrew Bible, which is based on a medieval text called the Leningrad Codex.

however, preserves a chiastic structure, where each grammatical element of the first line is repeated in reverse in the second line:

wə'ēlay	dāḇār	yəḡunnāḇ
to me	a word	it was secretly brought
(preposition pronoun)	(noun)	(verb)
wattiqqaḥ	'āzənî šêmeṣ	menhû
It received	my ear a whisper	from it
(verb)	(noun) (noun)	(preposition pronoun)

Thus, the order—prepositional phrase, noun, verb—is reversed in the second line with an added noun for clarification: verb, noun, noun, prepositional phrase. This is by no means the only example of a chiastic arrangement at the verse level, and in fact we can see the same organizational principle at work at the level of the entire book, where the center of the book is Job's two-pronged final defense: he meditates on the inscrutable nature of wisdom in chapter 28 and on the inscrutability of the meaning of Job's suffering in 29–31, highlighted by his reduction to "dust and ashes" in 30:19. Perceptive readers will notice that the phrase "dust and ashes" is repeated in Job's very last remarks of the book in 42:6 and will also notice that the "ashes" are what Job sits on in 2:8 after he is stricken with painful sores all over his body. In 2:12, Job's friends join him in his mourning by sprinkling "dust" on their heads. This chiastic arrangement is bookended by the narrator's description of Job as "blameless and upright" in 1:1 and that he dies "old and full of days" in 42:17. The significance of these two descriptions of Job relies on their similarity to descriptions of Abraham in Genesis. In Gen 17:1, 2 Yahweh tells Abram to "walk before [Yahweh] and be blameless. Then [Yahweh] will make [a] covenant between [the two of them] and will make [Abram] exceedingly numerous." Of course, the narrator of Job describes Job as having ten children and many livestock, indicating that Job and Yahweh have both, in a way, fulfilled their parts of the covenant of Abram. In Gen 25:8, Abraham dies an "old man and full of years": Job is described with the same phrase.[3]

Another indication of a chiastic arrangement of the book of Job is the repetition of Job as priest in 1:5 and 42:7–9. That is, Job mediates a sacrifice for his children in the opening chapter and does the same for his friends in the epilogue. The resulting chiastic structure is as follows[4]:

Chiastic Structure of the Book of Job

A: Job described as blameless and upright (1:1) (Abraham is called the same in Gen 17:1)

  B: Has much (1:2–3) Loses everything (1:13–22; 2:7)

    C: Described as a priest (1:5)

      D: On Dust and Ashes (2:8, 12)

        E: Decreation Monologue (3:1–26)

          F: Dialogues (4–27)

            G: Poem on Wisdom and Final Defense (28–31):

          Righteous, but not wise, like dust and ashes (30:19)

          F': Additional Dialogue/Elihu speeches (32–37)

        E': God's Speeches/Re-creation (38–41)

      D': Off Dust and Ashes (42:1–6)

    C': Described as priest (42:7–9)

  B': Restoration of belongings (42:10–15)

A': Dies old and content (compare to Abraham in Gen 25:8)

3. Hartley, *Book of Job*, 544.

4. A chiasm is traditionally ordered in such a way—A, B, C, C', B', A'—wherein the section marked A' parallels the section marked A, B' parallels B, and so forth.

APPROACHING JOB

One will notice that much of the way this structure breaks down is by smaller details in the prologue and epilogue, whereas the more conventional structure above breaks down the sections by chapter. Note, for instance, that in the second structure, God's speeches (E') are described as "re-creation," which work as reaction to the "decreation monologue" of Job's first speech in chapter 3 (E). In chapter 3, Job curses the day of his birth. By cursing this day, he calls for it essentially to be destroyed. In fact, in verse 4, Job parodies Gen 1:3, where God commences creation by saying, "Let there be light." In Job 3:4, Job calls for its destruction by saying, "Let it be darkness." The rest of the passage elaborates on the destruction of the light and other elements of that first day of Job's life. When Yahweh finally responds, thirty-four chapters later, his speech does not mention the friends. We know, however, that in 42:7-9, God rebukes the friends, saying they did not speak rightly concerning Yahweh, as Job did; God rebukes the friends despite initially ignoring the main arguments between Job and his friends. In fact, in the speeches from the tempest, Yahweh ignores Job's friends altogether, focusing entirely on Job. But instead of focusing on Job's complaints, Yahweh describes his creation, from the foundations of the earth to constellations to a litany of animals. Yahweh, perhaps, is re-creating the world in response to Job's decreation monologue,[5] leaving Elihu to respond to the dialogue between Job and his friends. Its chiastic arrangement makes Yahweh's response to chapter 3 clear.

What then stands out, given these elements of the structure, is that the arrangement centers on G (30:19), which points back to D (2:8, 12) / D' (42:1-6). In a modern Western structuralist sense, Job's final defense is an apt hinge for the narrative of the book of Job. After a mysterious

---

5. Alter, *Wisdom Books*, 158.

Structure and Critical Issues

poem on the elusive nature of wisdom, Job gives one last argument directly to God, desiring no more mediation from his friends. Keeping an eye on the chiasm at play, we see that right in the middle of his speech (30:19) Job points back to the dust and ashes of the prologue (2:8, 12), declaring that God has thrown him to the mud, reducing him to dust and ashes—a symbol of mourning and grief. In short, Job has become the symbol upon which he lies.

I will add more details to the exegesis of 42:1–6 in chapter 3. What follows highlights how the structure can aid in exegesis. After Yahweh responds to Job's first speech, Job replies in 42:1–6, concluding with what the NRSV translates as "therefore I despise myself and repent in dust and ashes." This verse has caused a lot of controversy since the Hebrew is very unconventional. Unlike Job 4:12 cited above, where Eliphaz offers two parallel sentences with a verb in both clauses, 42:6 has Job place two verbs in the first section of the verse and a prepositional phrase containing two nouns in the second. A literal translation of the phrase would be something like, "Therefore, I reject and regret upon dust and ashes." Of course this translation makes little sense, since both verbs—"reject" (*m's*) and "regret" (*nḥm* in the *niphal* stem)—are missing direct objects. Most translations join the NRSV in providing a reflexive direct object for "reject" (thus, "despise myself") and in maintaining the primary meaning for the preposition *'al* ("upon"). However, the chiastic structure can aid us in determining a translation more appropriate to the narrative of the book as a whole.

If one views the book of Job as following a chiastic trajectory, one will notice that the book begins by describing Job like Abram/Abraham and that the book ends by describing Job like Abram/Abraham. Job begins the story with ten children and much livestock, and ends with ten children and much livestock. Job is described as a priest at the beginning and at the end. It would make little sense, then, for Job to sit on ashes (2:8) *after* being established as Abrahamic, wealthy, and priestly, and *remain* on ashes (42:6) while performing the duties of a priest. The chiastic structure suggests that the narrative reverses (so to speak) and that Job becomes as he was *before* he sat on the ashes in 2:8.

Such a reading of the text would be moot if the verse in question unambiguously means "therefore I despise myself and repent in dust and ashes." Fortunately, as I describe in more detail in chapter 3, a valid, if wordy, rendering of 42:6 is, "Therefore, I retract [my argument] and have completed the rites of mourning upon dust and ashes."[6] In such a translation, "reject" (*m's*), following the "therefore," refers to previous words (as in Isa 30:12) and "repent upon" (*nḥm 'al*) means "complete the rites of mourning" (as it does in Jer 31:15).[7] After making such a declaration, Job is now in the right state to perform his priestly duties for his friends and die old and contented, and those of us paying attention to structure can rest contented at the tidiness of the book.

To sum up, viewing the structure of the book of Job as chiastic supports such a reading. Not only does an awareness of structure give readers some perspective on how the narrative works, but it also illumines some sections and may even aid in translating difficult verses. The book of Job is the story of a righteous man who loses everything and then, though this point is often neglected, gains it back.

---

6. One can see why modern English Bibles prefer a shorter and more poetic translation, but the meaning of the traditional translations is so counter to the likely meaning of the verse that such renderings are hardly justifiable.

7. See also Isa 57:6; Jer 8:6; 18:8, 10; Joel 2:13; Amos 7:3, 6; Jonah 3:10; 4:2; 1 Chr 21:15.

Structure and Critical Issues

Paying attention to the structure between the beginning and end helps shed light on a long and complicated story.

Of course, nothing is quite as simple as it seems at first. For instance, some may argue that the above structures are irrelevant due to the structures assuming the integrity of the book. In other words, what if the book were really just a composite of passages by a disparate group of writers working in different contexts in different eras? Can we even posit a unified or unifying structure of the book of Job like either of those above if there is no "book of Job"? The following section discusses these problems.

CRITICAL ISSUES REGARDING THE BOOK OF JOB

It is customary for biblical scholars (particularly authors of commentaries, a category of work to which this book does not belong) to list critical details of a given biblical book. These details include the composition date, the book's author, and the text's integrity or lack thereof. I have held off on presenting these details up until now because I do not believe them to be important in engaging with the text of the book of Job, as evidenced by the history of the book's reception, mainly by people who had no knowledge of or interest in the critical history of the book. And yet the book of Job spoke to them in powerful ways—indeed, usually more powerfully than to those who become preoccupied in the history behind the text.

Still, there is some use to knowing about the composition history of the book. As we were detailing the characters of the book in the previous chapter, certain questions about consistency kept arising. Why is *hassatan* never mentioned after the second chapter? Why are there different uses of the divine name in the different sections of the book? Why does Zophar only have two speeches while the other friends have three? What is the deal with Elihu? Thinking through these questions in light of other evidence can give readers more confidence in interpretation and can help eliminate flawed readings. The process may also highlight areas in the book that deserve more attention. For instance, having an idea of when the book of Job was written may help some interpreters determine a reason for writing the book of Job in the first place, which may illumine the meaning of the book.

Date

Despite a few holdouts, most scholars believe that the book of Job is a relatively late book in the Hebrew canon. This has not always been the case. In fact, many have presumed Job to be the oldest book in the Bible, a sentiment that continues in at least some cultures. After telling people that I work on the book of Job, often someone will say (sometimes in the form of a question) that the book of Job is the oldest in the Bible. I have countered with evidence I will introduce below, and the person who raised the subject of Job's composition date will respond with a look that betrays a cross between disbelief and offense, acting quickly to change the subject.

    I suspect that behind the belief about the antiquity of the book of Job is a confusion between the setting of the story and the date of its authorship. Job the character is indeed early and has much in common with the patriarchs of Genesis.[8] As I mentioned in the previous chapter, Job

8. Due to the appearance of Job in the book of Ezekiel (14:14, 19), we can presume that the legend of Job preceded the book of Job by several centuries. Perhaps, even, the prologue of Job existed in some cursory form before its reworking for what would become the canonized book.

Structure and Critical Issues

is meant to be compared to Abraham and Adam. Also, he performs priestly duties outside of a centralized system, which was not developed until Israel settled in the land of Canaan. However, this does not mean that the author of the book of Job has any proximity with the setting, whether of time or place. Even if Moses wrote the book of Job, as some have argued,[9] that would still place the authorship over one thousand years after Job's supposed lifetime, according to most timelines. Let us then proceed with evidence within the book to determine a more plausible date of authorship.

There really is no reason to think that the book of Job precedes the Babylonian exile. The book of Job does not discuss historical details like other books of the Bible, so finding an earliest date is much more difficult than in a book like Jeremiah, which describes details that led to the Babylonian exile. However, the book of Job shares a lot of language with the book of Jeremiah, particularly with those passages called the laments of Jeremiah. Most strikingly compare Jeremiah 20:14–18 to Job 3:3–4, 11–12:

> Cursed be the day
> > on which I was born!
> The day when my mother bore me,
> > let it not be blessed!
> Cursed be the man
> > who brought the news to my father, saying,
> "A child is born to you, a son,"
> > making him very glad.
> Let that man be like the cities

---

9. *b. Baba Batra* 14b; Young, *Introduction*, 319–23; R. Laird Harris, "Doctrine of God in Job," 156; etc. See also Robert Lowth (1710–1787), who popularized the early date of Job based on the language of the text. We will see below how his thesis is complicated by other internal data.

> that the Lord overthrew without pity;
> let him hear a cry in the morning
> > and an alarm at noon,
> because he did not kill me in the womb;
> > so my mother would have been my grave,
> > and her womb forever great.
> Why did I come forth from the womb
> > to see toil and sorrow,
> > and spend my days in shame? (Jer 20:14–18)

> "Let the day perish in which I was born,
> > and the night that said,
> > 'A man-child is conceived.'
> Let that day be darkness!
> > May God above not seek it,
> > or light shine on it . . .

> "Why did I not die at birth,
> > come forth from the womb and expire?
> Why were there knees to receive me,
> > or breasts for me to suck? (Job 3:3–4, 11–12)

Though we cannot be sure if Jeremiah influenced Job or if Job influenced Jeremiah (and there are other instances of similar speech between the two books),[10] it seems more likely that the author of Job would have heightened the speeches of Jeremiah than that Jeremiah would have muted those of Job.

Job, in fact, shares much in common with other famous sufferers besides Jeremiah in the Hebrew Bible, most notably the author of Lamentations and the Suffering

---

10. Job 19:7 and Jer 20:8; Job 19:24 and Jer 17:1; and Job 21:7–20 and Jer 12:1–3.

Structure and Critical Issues

Servant of Isaiah.[11] Because Lamentations and Second Isaiah were written between the destruction of Jerusalem (586 BCE) and the fall of Babylon (539 BCE), it is safe to argue that Job emerges sometime around the fall of Babylon in the mid-sixth century.

Also consider the same passage from Job 3:3 (lit. "that day, let it be darkness") and how it parodies Gen 1:3 ("Let there be light"). It is possible that Genesis parodies Job, but given the influence of Genesis throughout the canon, it is more likely that Job is the later book. If we also include Job's comparisons to Abraham and Adam (as described in chapter 2 below), the evidence seems to point to Genesis being the influence and Job the influenced.

Beyond Genesis and Jeremiah, Job parodies psalms, most famously Psalm 8, where the psalmist writes:

> what are human beings that you are mindful of them,
>> mortals that you care for them?
> Yet you have made them a little lower than God,
>> and crowned them with glory and honor.
>> (Ps 8:4, 5)

In Job 7, Job says:

> What are human beings, that you make so much of them,
>> that you set your mind on them,
> visit them every morning,
>> test them every moment?
> Will you not look away from me for a while,

---

11. See Seow, *Job 1–21*, 42, (who cites Job 9:8a and Isa 44:24c; Job 12:9b and Isa 41:20a; Job 16:17a and Isa 53:9b; Job 26:12a and Isa 51:15b; Job 6:4, Job 7:20, and Lam 3:12; Job 9:18b and Lam 3:15a; Job 12:4 and Lam 3:14; Job 16:9–10 and Lam 2:16; Job 16:12 and Lam 3:12; Job 19:7–8 and Lam 3:7–9; Job 30:9 and Lam 3:14) for a longer analysis of these two comparisons.

let me alone until I swallow my spittle?
(Job 7:17–19)

In Job 3, Job parodies Gen 1:3 by reversing the meaning. In Job 7, he maintains the meaning of Psalm 8, but reverses the sentiment. Again, we cannot know whether Job borrowed from the psalm or the psalmist borrowed from Job or they both borrowed from an independent, nonbiblical source, but it seems more likely that Job is negatively parodying Psalm 8 more than Psalm 8 putting a positive spin on a negative text.

That Job has an intertextual relationship with these other biblical books does not lead us very far in our quest to determine its date (though I have included the parallels above for their interpretive value beyond dating and provenance). But there are other clues that lead us to think that Job was completed in the Persian era (539–330 BCE). These are made up mainly of small details. We discussed in the previous chapter the similarity between *hassatan* in Job 1–2 and a brief appearance of what seems to be the same character in Zech 3:1–2, written between 520 and 518 BCE. In the poetry of Job 19:24, which introduces the famous phrase "I know that my Redeemer lives," Job says, "O that with an iron pen and with lead [my words] were engraved on a rock forever!" which bears a striking similarity to an inscription commissioned by Darius I a mere two decades after the fall of Babylon and only around five years after Zechariah was active.[12] Based on these and other minor details, a Persian-era composition seems more likely than not.

However, we must also consider the language employed by the poet in determining date, for it was the language of Job that drew Robert Lowth to hypothesize that Job was the oldest book in the Hebrew Bible. In contrast to Lowth, Robert Alter notes that the language indicates

---

12. Seow, *Job 1–21*, 802–3.

Structure and Critical Issues

a later date, likely from the late sixth century to as late as the fourth century BCE. For one, Job shares Hebrew words that appear only outside of Job in Esther and Chronicles. Second, the poet employs some morphological quirks and vocabulary from Aramaic that suggest to Alter that the poet likely heard "a good deal of Aramaic all around him and probably actively spoke it himself together with Hebrew," placing the author well after the destruction of Jerusalem by the Aramaic-speaking Babylonians and the subsequent sacking of Babylon by the Aramaic-speaking western Persians.[13]

Employing a similar linguistic analysis to Alter's, Newsom, following most of the important critical commentators of the nineteenth and twentieth centuries,[14] argues that the Elihu speeches differ in language and style from those of the other speeches. Further, the absence of any mention of Elihu outside of the speeches helps posit an even later date for Elihu's insertion into the text.[15] Due to similarities between Job and the deuterocanonical book Wisdom of Sirach, in particular, Newsom posits a qualified date range for Elihu in the late Persian or early Hellenistic era.

In any case, one cannot engrave a date for Job or Elihu in a rock forever, so to speak. Many respected scholars differ in their hypotheses, and several important commentators continue to differ in their analyses about the date of the book. In fact, determining the date of the book of Job has little bearing on the interpretation of the book. However, exploring the details that lead to a hypothetical date does have value beyond the date itself. That is, examining Job's intertextual relationship with other biblical texts reveals the richness of the book of Job. The process may also reveal

13. Alter, *Wisdom Books*, 4–5.
14. Namely, Dhorme, Driver and Gray, and Pope.
15. Newsom, *Book of Job*, 204.

other critical issues that have led to bigger problems for interpreters, which we explore below.

Critical Issues in the Book of Job

When exploring the date of the book of Job, what one generally means is the date of the final form of the book (perhaps, minus Elihu). What one cannot determine with any accuracy at all is the date of any early versions of the book of Job that have been used by the final editor, or even if there are such earlier versions. It does seem reasonable to presume a more complicated timeline than the one described above.

Consider the following: A non-Israelite named Job, known for his wealth and virtue, suffers a great calamity, inspiring a legend passed down orally for centuries. Because he is not an Israelite or does not encounter characters in the history of Israel, the biblical writers make no mention of him until Ezekiel includes him in a group of righteous men of legend (14:20). A century later, a sage and poet takes a version of the legend, in which the character of Job loses much and regains it later, and expands the story to include a wager in heaven between *hassatan* and God, as well as a series of theological dialogues between Job and the friends who come to comfort him. The result is the majority of the text we have today, minus the hymn to Wisdom (chapter 28), speeches by Elihu (chapters 32–37) and Yahweh's second speech (chapters 40–41). Over the course of the next several decades, another sage adds a wisdom poem that suggests wisdom is ungraspable by humanity; a "dissatisfied reader" inserts further discussion into the text—ideas and arguments not included by the original poet: this reader adds these new ideas through the creation of a new character—Elihu—and another poet adds a second speech for

Structure and Critical Issues

Yahweh. After either the last of these poets or another editor completes this final version of the book of Job, some scribes copy passages of the book incorrectly. Other passages are omitted altogether. So we must consider these losses in our readings today while reconstructing the original text as well as we can.

The above hypothetical timeline should not be considered definitive, but rather a possible history of the text of Job from its origins to its form adopted in the canon. Here I delve a little more deeply into the evidence we have of the corruptions and lacunae described in the last sentence of the above timeline.

The most obvious place to start is noting the discrepancies between the prose prologue and the poetic dialogues, not the least of which is the generic differences themselves. A simple folktale and a sophisticated poem seem unlikely (though not impossible) to have been produced by the same writer. Beyond genre, though, the prose sections use a different vocabulary from the poetic ones. Most significantly, the prose prologue and epilogue refer to the deity by the Tetragrammaton while the dialogues are largely bereft of the name Yahweh. Instead, Job and his friends use different names for God like *'el*, *'eloah*, and *shaddai*. When "Yahweh" does appear in the dialogues, it is in the prose sections that introduce the divine speeches from the tempest or in other contested passages, presenting evidence of editorial additions to these sections.[16] Also consider how few specifics about Job's suffering appear in the poetry. The bulk of the book says little about the nature of Job's losses, mentions little about his children or wife, and offers little about Job's physical trials. In the poetry, Job's losses stem from decreased social standing rather than from physical

---

16. Lawrie, *How Critical*, 127.

adversity. Yet the prose prologue gives no indication that Job suffered socially at all.

Within the dialogues themselves, many scholars have argued that the third cycle of speeches in chapters 24–27 shows signs of corrupted scribal transmissions that "may have been made deliberately in order to confuse the issue and nullify Job's argument."[17] Why would someone purposefully jumble these speeches? Could it be that the already borderline blasphemous Job actually crosses the line in the missing speech? Could an early scribe who could tolerate Job's first two cycles of complaints have felt that the last response to Zophar could not remain in the text? Did this scribe move some verses around during his transmission and omit Job's final speech altogether?

While the first two dialogue cycles have speeches in the order Eliphaz-Job-Bildad-Job-Zophar-Job, the third cycle interrupts the pattern. Bildad's speech is only five verses long, and Zophar's is entirely absent. Even more curious, the speech in chapter 26, which is marked in the text as Job's, sounds more like a speech from one of the friends. The speaker remarks at the power and mystery of God in the world rather than complaining about or lamenting Job's condition. Several scholars have surmised that chapter 26 has been mislabeled as Job's. Rather, the words should be considered Bildad's shortened speech. Alternatively, the introduction should introduce an omitted speech by Job while the included speech (mislabeled as Job's) should be considered the words of Zophar. Other scholars have undertaken an involved reconstruction of the text so that Bildad's, Job's, and Zophar's speeches look quite different from the received Masoretic Text but fit the antecedent themes

17. Pope, *Job*, xx.

Structure and Critical Issues

and tones of the first two cycles. For instance, Samuel Terrien[18] offers the following hypothetical reconstruction:

Third Speech of Eliphaz	22:1–30
Job's Reply	23:1—24:17, 25
Third Speech of Bildad	25:1–6; 26:5–14
Job's Reply	26:1–4; 27:1–12
Third Speech of Zophar	24:18–24; 27:13–23
Job's Reply	now missing

Other hypothetical reconstructions are similar.[19] In the above reconstruction, Zophar speaks the words attributed to Job in chapters 24 and 27 that praise the reliability of God's justice and the destiny of the wicked (24:18–24 and 27:13–23), Bildad elaborates on the worm theology on which he waxes in chapter 25 with 26:5–14, and Job's reply to Zophar is missing altogether.

Complicating matters even further, immediately following the end of chapter 27 comes a poem on wisdom, also without a prose introduction. Though the poem has been praised for its language, it does not obviously fit well in the mouths of any of the participants of the dialogue. Furthermore, both chapters 27 and 29 open with the phrase, "Job again took up his discourse and said," suggesting that chapter 28 interrupts Job's speech rather than comes from the mouth of Job. The conclusion that many have posited is that chapter 28 is a later addition by an unknown author and with an unknown speaker who is offering another point of view on the matter.[20]

---

18. Terrien, *Poet of Existence*, 34.

19. E.g., Pope, *Job*, xx; and Clines, *Job 21–37*, 618–28, 641–44, and 651–63.

20. Newsom, *Book of Job*, 171–72.

Similarly, as I noted above, the speeches of Elihu (chapters 32–37) were potentially appended to the book of Job at a later date, likely in the later Persian or early Hellenistic era. Elihu is never mentioned as having been present during the prologue or three speech cycles between Job and his friends and seems to repeat many of the friends' arguments. His vocabulary also differs from that of the other participants in the dialogues. For instance, Elihu favors using the divine name *'ēl* while Job and his friends favor *'elôah*. Also, like *hassatan*, once Elihu ceases speaking he disappears entirely from the narrative. The inclusion of the character of Elihu in the book of Job remains the biggest problem for those seeking to secure the "original text" of the book.

Finally, Yahweh's second speech (40:6—41:34), which has been called inferior to his first speech, comes after Job's humble response in 40:4-5, and has been characterized as "nagging," so it too may have been a late addition to the final text of the book of Job.[21]

Arguments for the General Integrity of the Book of Job

The above comments represent the results of source and form-critical analyses, but many of the conclusions of such analyses have been challenged in recent scholarship. Advances in poetics, structural analysis, and literary approaches have led a growing number of scholars to argue for the overall integrity of the book of Job, largely as received in the Hebrew text.[22] What follows is a summary of potential answers to the questions about the integrity of the book:

21. Rowley, *Job*, 254.

22. Among important commentators who vouch for integrity in most cases, see Habel, Newsom, Janzen, Seow, and Fokkelman.

Structure and Critical Issues

Regarding *hassatan*, his initial two attacks on Job set up a thought experiment that the remainder of the book tests. His role in the story is complete after the second attack on Job's body, so mention of him after chapter 2 would not contribute to what the book of Job sets out to do.[23] Also, while generic differences between prose and poetry account partly for the ostensible discrepancies between the narrative and the dialogues, the use of a prose frame narrative surrounding poetic dialogue has precedence in ancient southwest Asia—particularly in Egyptian wisdom literature.[24]

As I indicated in the previous chapter, the third dialogue cycle, as received, reflects a disintegration of the conversation between Job and his three friends.[25] Zophar's impatience leads him to cease speaking at all, and Job's speech ironically employs the likely words of Zophar, in recognition that he is paying attention but does not agree with Job. Chapter 28 should then be considered a speech by Job and acts as his response to his friends' feeble arguments about their own presuppositions. The final verse of chapter 28 repeats the narrator's language that describes Job in the opening verses of the book (that Job feared the Lord and turned away from evil). This repeated language carries Job's assessment of his experience in suffering and of his friends' responses to his complaints.

While even several proponents of the integrity of the book of Job find Elihu's inclusion suspect, Elihu is not controversial to many in the history of Job interpretation. John Calvin, for instance, regards Elihu as an important contributor to the discussion and notes that he is never rebuked

23. Walton with Vizcaino, *Job*, 26.

24. Seow, *Job 1–21*, 27–28.

25. Janzen, *Job*, 172ff.; cf. Seow, *Job 1–21*, 29–30; and Lawrie, "How Critical," 132–33.

by God, so his words should be taken seriously, if not definitively. More recently, Seow argues that Elihu should be considered a representative of the Elistic tradition—the tradition that places the god El highest among Canaanite gods. Ezekiel and Daniel, who believe that divine revelation comes through an intermediary and by means of dreams and visions, also represent the Elistic tradition.[26] Elihu, therefore, as a mediator for God acts as a proper antecedent to Yahweh's direct communication immediately following.

As for Yahweh's nagging in chapters 40 and 41, well, whether the speech is nagging seems mainly a matter of opinion. While some find Yahweh relentless in berating Job, others find great meaning in the introduction of and litany on the Behemoth and Leviathan.

Jan Fokkelman applies a poetic analysis based on meter that he has tested on other biblical texts. Though his method has been criticized for being too rigid in its use of counting syllables, it has allowed him to offer another reason to accept the text of Job in its final form. Based on his poetic analysis, Fokkelman has determined that Job's words make up exactly half of all the poetry in the dialogues, inclusive of all the disputed sections. So Fokkelman concludes that the poem is purposely constructed to the syllable in the form we have (though without vowel markings).[27]

Furthermore, no extant versions of Job, not even the Targum and old Greek versions, corroborate any of the historical-critical hypotheses. Many have noted that the old Greek version of Job, found in LXX, is one-sixth shorter than the Hebrew version, and that the Vulgate and Syriac versions are also shorter.[28] However, these versions are

26. Seow, *Job 1–21*, 34.

27. Fokkelman, *Book of Job in Form*, 8.

28. "The translator's own footprint—indeed, the tread on [the Greek writer's] shoes—occupies an equal or larger space in Iob [*sic*]

shorter within the different sections of poetry and are not missing any major section, such as any Elihu or Yahweh speeches. Rather, it is more likely that the difficulty of the poetic syntax in the book of Job (especially the use of ellipses as in other Northwest Semitic poetry but not in Indo-European poetry) inspired the Greek and Latin scribes to simplify their translations for their respective audiences.[29]

Currently no scholarly consensus exists about the composition history of the book of Job, but the trend is moving toward the overall integrity of the book. An integral and unified text of Job is potentially reassuring to many readers of Scripture. However, if in the next generation scholars swing back to a complex history of composition along with a hopelessly corrupt final product, the book of Job as received will likely remain, as it has for centuries, a powerful text to many people. It is the final form that has inspired a multitude of interpretations and applications, and the final form will likely continue to do so. The next chapter will highlight many of these interpretations, paying attention to things like hermeneutical strategy and theological presuppositions. However, as we will see, historical criticism does still have bearing on some interpretations.

---

than anywhere else in the LXX corpus" (Cox, "*Ipsissima verba*"). It goes beyond the scope of this book to detail the role of the Greek Job in the book of Job's reception, so a further quote from Cox's paper will suffice: In discussing the *additions* in the Greek Job in the Septuagint, Cox writes, "No addition is longer than a line and they serve various purposes. The dominant purposes seem to stem from a desire to provide emphasis, clarification, and vividness to the discussions. [The Greek writer's] use of rare words reflects the mind of an intellectual who has an interest in Job as a literary document. While generally aspiring to 'good Greek,' [the Greek writer] is not above introducing Hebraisms into the translation. These, as additions (and translation), lend a familiarity to the text from the standpoint of readers who skew the LXX and its underlying source text."

29. Althann, "Reflections on the Text of the Book of Job," 8.

REVIEW QUESTIONS

1. Compare and contrast the two structures of Job offered above.

2. How does outlining the structure of the book of Job affect how one reads the book?

3. Does it matter to modern readers if the book of Job was written by a single author or not? How would one's reading of Job change to presuppose that the book is the work of several authors and an editor who stitched it together into what we have today?

3

MEANING IN INDIVIDUAL PASSAGES

FINDING MEANING IN THE BOOK OF JOB

Though many have resigned themselves to understanding Job as a diverse book with a complex prehistory, such a compositional background has not stopped people from finding meaning in the book. For some who hold a high view of Scripture, the mere inclusion of Job in the Bible would be enough to warrant theological reflection. The difficulties in interpretation due to a questionable compositional background would not hinder reflection for those who view the Bible as infallible or inspired of God. However, a glance at the diverse backgrounds of Job's interpreters (Catholic, Protestant, Jewish, Muslim, liberal, evangelical, agnostic, atheistic) proves that even a complex prehistory does not hinder deep reflection of the text. Perhaps the subject of unjust suffering, coupled with a curious or even opaque ending of such a long book has inspired the challenge of finding the meaning of the book and, in some cases, meaning in one's own suffering. The messiness of the book of Job mirrors the messiness of life itself, which may be as inspiring as anything else in the book.

In this chapter, we will tackle theological and academic responses to Job. How have academics and other scholarly minded writers gone about finding meaning in Job? In particular, what strategies are employed to search for the central message of the book? Different views of Job's central message often arise because progenitors and their followers focus on key passages. Interpreters tend to highlight particular chapters or verses in Job and use them as lenses through which to read the rest of the book. Because some of these interpretations come in the midst of a commentary on the whole book of Job, the interpreters do not consciously marginalize other parts of Job, but they do in some way lessen the impact of the texts that do not contribute to their overarching thesis about the book of Job. This is not a fault, necessarily. There may well be secondary motifs in the book of Job that enhance the main thesis but are not the main point themselves. Of course, however persuasive Eliphaz and his friends are during their speeches, very few commentators consider what they say to be authoritative by the time Yahweh pronounces their words wrong in chapter 42. Whatever a given interpreter believes the message of Job to be will influence which passages this interpreter marginalizes or favors.

Below, and in the order they appear within the book of Job, I will spend time examining individual passages central to separate interpretations of the book. All these passages are controversial, either for historical-critical reasons (detailed in chapter 2) or for translation reasons or for theological reasons.

Meaning in Individual Passages

Job 1:9 ("Then Satan answered the Lord, "Does Job fear God for nothing?")

When *hassatan* visits Yahweh in the divine court, Yahweh begins by asking questions. "Where have you come from?" he asks first (1:7); and then, "Have you considered my servant Job? There is no one like him on the earth, a blameless and upright man who fears God and turns away from evil" (1:8). *Hassatan*, perhaps foreshadowing Yahweh's response to Job from the tempest, responds to Yahweh with rhetorical questions. "Does Job fear God for nothing (*ḥinnam*)? Have you not put a fence around him and his house and all that he has, on every side? You have blessed the work of his hands, and his possessions have increased in the land. But stretch out your hand now, and touch all that he has, and he will curse you to your face" (1:9–11). That is, is Job's famous piety merely part of an economy where Job gives much in the way of service and sacrifice in response to God's protecting him from calamity and providing him with many children and much land and livestock? One can test this piety if all the reasons for it are taken away.

The rest of the prologue bears out the consequences of *hassatan*'s musings. Job loses all the things that may have contributed to his service and sinlessness, but he still "holds onto his integrity" (cf. 2:9–10; see 1:22).

If one were to see this passage as the central question of the book, whether it is possible for someone to devote him- or herself to God disinterestedly, then how does the rest of the book bear this out? The retributive theology of the friends is seen through this lens: Just as *hassatan* argues that Job serves God because God has given him much, the friends argue the inverse: God has punished Job for having been impious. Thus, through this lens, the friends are seen as especially devious, taking the side of God's adversary, in at least a correlative manner. They are, in a manner of speaking, devil's advocates, and their punishment in the epilogue seems well deserved, until we think of the argument laid out in the book—that piety should be disinterested and that God is a free agent who does not work within a human-produced system.

The theology of the book, then, when seen through this passage, is a theology of freedom. True piety is disinterested and freely bestowed, because God is a truly free God, free to bestow grace and mercy outside any system of human construction.

Though people concerned about justice may be troubled by aspects of this thesis, any objective observer of the way the world really does work must confront the reality to which Job admits early in his suffering: "Do not human beings have a hard service on earth, / and are not their days like the days of a laborer?" (7:1). The innocent do suffer, which raises the question of the worthiness of God for our worship and calls for a theology that recognizes God's freedom. Preeminent liberation theologian Gustavo Gutiérrez is one theologian who reads Job through the lens of *hassatan*'s question:

> Is it possible to believe in God without expectation of reward, or 'for nothing'? In an effort to answer this question the poet comes upon the doctrine of temporal retribution. This, he finds, does not take into account his own experience or the experience of so many others. He therefore looks for a correct way of talking about God within the most strained and knotty of all human situations: the suffering of the innocent.[1]

The result of attempting to answer the question through the rest of the book of Job is a dramatic model for those

1. Gutiérrez, *On Job*, 93.

Meaning in Individual Passages

who do care about innocent suffering. "Job shows us a way," Gutiérrez writes, "with his vigorous protest, his discovery of concrete commitment to the poor and all who suffer unjustly, his facing up to God, and his acknowledgment of the gratuitousness that characterizes God's plan for human history."[2]

Job 1:21–22 (He said, "Naked I came from my mother's womb, and naked shall I return there; the LORD gave, and the LORD has taken away; blessed be the name of the LORD." In all this Job did not sin or charge God with wrongdoing.)

When people discuss the "patience of Job," they most likely think of the proverb that Job either quotes or coins in 1:21. When Job loses everything he has, which is substantial, he does not at first get angry or seek revenge but recognizes that all is a gift. In the two direct allusions to Job in the rest of the Bible, this picture of Job seems most evident. In Ezekiel 14, the legendary Job is included with Noah and Daniel as uniquely righteous characters, able to save themselves during a plague of God-ordained punishment. Perhaps Ezekiel had in mind a Job who, like Noah, witnessed a world collapsing around him while only he survived due to his righteousness. The other biblical allusion to Job comes from James 5:11, which has been traditionally translated, "You have heard of the patience of Job," but which the NRSV translates as "the endurance of Job," reflecting better the Job of the entire book rather than of just the prologue. Many have suggested, however, that James did not have the entire book in mind, but just the prologue, and that 1:21 offers the best example of the Job James knew, since Job's immediate response to his sufferings seems remarkable. However, if one understands, as the NRSV does, that *hupomone* refers

2. Ibid., 102.

to enduring,³ and that Jas 5:11 is concerned with the telos of the Lord for Job, then perhaps James's interpretation has some justification, even given the scope of the entire book of Job.⁴ One must still account for Job's speeches, which hardly seem patient towards God, and especially for chapter 3, which even stretches the meaning of endurance, considering Job's desire never to have been born, which we will discuss more below.

One of Søren Kierkegaard's "Upbuilding Discourses" focuses on Job 1:20, 21. Kierkegaard observes that Job places both credit and blame for his wealth and losses, respectively, on God. Job ignores the ostensible actors of his losses—Chaldeans and Sabeans—and sees God as the agent. The Lord was the agent of Job's wealth and so, therefore, Job can hardly remain upset when he loses it all since it is as if he is returning items on loan from God: "It was as if it were not the Lord who took it away but Job who gave it back to him."⁵ Of course, seven days later Job has a different response. He curses the day of his birth and desires never to have been born. As human drama, Job's change of heart rings true. The initial response of a truly pious man would probably be as Kierkegaard describes it; yet even a pious man succumbs to frustration as he mulls over his situation while no action happens in response.

On the other hand, in the dialogues, Job does not argue with his friends' retributive theology in a way congruous to his words in 1:21. Rather than arguing with his friends from a fundamental philosophical level—that God is free and that suffering does not correspond to actions—he argues that the system into which he had bought in the past

---

3. Other translations have "steadfastness" (ESV) and "perseverance" (NIV).

4. See Seitz, "Patience of Job in the Epistle of James," 373–82.

5. Kierkegaard, *Discourses*, 116–17.

is broken. In Job 9:17, Job says, "For he crushes me with a tempest, / and multiplies my wounds without cause." Some would argue that this hardly sounds like the same Job as the one in 1:21, but tellingly 9:17 points back to the words of *hassatan* in 1:9, who uses the word *ḥinnam* to question Job's piety. Here, Job alludes to the divine wager, accusing God of attacking him for nothing (*ḥinnam*). The allusion gives the critic pause in analyzing the history of a simple text. Job is a profoundly complex character who develops a theology over time. We can even say something similar about his friends.

Job 3–27 (The Debate)

While the book of Job begins with Job's great losses and suffering, the center and bulk of the book is made up of a debate between four friends. As I mentioned previously, the specifics of Job's sufferings go either unmentioned in the dialogues or obscured by the length of the dialogues and the details that Job and his friends bat back and forth. Though Bildad brings up Job's children and their punishment in chapter 8, the majority of the speeches throughout the dialogues seem to have little to do directly with the prologue.

Though the debate takes up roughly 60 percent of the book, some interpreters might forgive those who dismiss its relevance entirely and skip to the end where a pronouncement comes from an infallible God. Further, that word from God declares the words of the friends to be mistaken, making the debate not merely irrelevant but counterproductive to right theology. Nevertheless, many in the history of interpretation have found the debate instructive in a variety of ways.

One common interpretive strategy views the friends' arguments as allegories of current ideological arguments. Maimonides, for instance, views Job as "keeping with the opinion of Aristotle; the opinion of Eliphaz is in keeping with the opinion of our Law; the opinion of Bildad is in keeping with the doctrine of the Mu'tazila; the opinion of Zophar is in keeping with the doctrine of the Ash'ariyya."[6]

Before Maimonides, Saadiah identifies the friends as Christian and Muslim detractors of Judaism.[7] In the twentieth-century play *J. B.*, Archibald MacLeish turns Eliphaz, Bildad, and Zophar into a psychiatrist, a Marxist, and a priest, respectively.[8] Thus, Job and his friends have inspired readers across the centuries to seek meaning in their debate relevant to their current context.

Some readings have found meaning not only in the content of the dialogue but in the dialogue itself. Thomas Aquinas, for instance, recognizes the debate as eventually subsuming the story to the point that "chief among Job's adversities, as it were, was that he had been deserted by his friends."[9] Similar to (even influenced by) Maimonides, Aquinas views the debate as a *disputatio*, a formal academic debate used in medieval Europe.[10] Despite the obvious anachronism, Aquinas makes some observations that are worth considering. Primarily, by viewing the debate thus, Thomas questions the effectiveness of Job's rhetoric,

---

6. Maimonides, *Guide of the Perplexed*, 494.

7. Larrimore, *Book of Job*, 87.

8. However, they only appear in the play for roughly 10 percent of the performance, suggesting MacLeish finds the debate of minor importance in the book of Job. Also, the play is not so much an interpretation of Job as an appropriation of it.

9. Saint Thomas Aquinas, *Job*, 472.

10. See Yaffe, "Interpretive Essay," 25–28.

Meaning in Individual Passages

concluding that Job may have sinned (ironically) in the process of arguing his innocence.[11]

Carol Newsom calls the book of Job a "contest of moral imaginations" wherein the characters' different arguments make up the point of the story. Using the Bakhtinian category of polyphony, Newsom explores how meaning can be approached without reducing the characters and their points of view to props or straw men, which merely draw readers to a definitive conclusion that matches that of the author. Instead, truth exists through the dynamic of the dialogue itself, "at the point of intersection of several unmerged voices" and not through a particular point of view. We are not accustomed to listening for truth at such an intersection of voices.[12] However, the friends are, after all, not straw men but often speak well about God in ways that befuddle commentators who know that God will eventually declare the friends' words wrong.[13] Likewise, Job comes so close to blasphemy that commentators have had difficulty reconciling Job's speeches with his eventual redemption.[14] Viewing the book of Job as a polyphonic text allows the characters to be more fully incarnated and to show the complexity of truth itself. Such a view invites readers into

11. Ibid., 27.

12. Newsom, *Book of Job*, 22.

13. In fact, even the apostle Paul quotes Eliphaz (Job 5:13) favorably in 1 Cor 3:19, which should, perhaps, be seen as a credit to Eliphaz and not a demerit on Paul.

14. For example, John Calvin says of Job in his sermon on Job 23:1–7, "Certainly [Job] does not [speak rightly], for he speaks excessively . . . Job, then supposes that God uses toward him an absolute power as it is called; that is, 'I am God and I will do whatever will seem good to me although it has no form of justice. I will act with an excessive domination.' But here *Job blasphemes God* . . . Our Lord cannot be more powerful than he is just; his justice and power are inseparable" [italics added]; quoted in Schreiner, *Where Shall Wisdom Be Found?*, 114.

the dialogue with the friends. Perhaps, as Newsom suggests, the inclusion of Elihu is evidence that just such a person took it upon him- or herself to join the conversation in the guise of Elihu after the dialogue had seemingly been finalized.

If Elihu's speeches are in fact a later addition to the book of Job, brought on by someone drawn into the debate itself, only the book's subsequent canonization has really kept others from also entering the fray. Debate as a main point of the book of Job has essentially been allegorized in its history of interpretation. Because of the multiplicity of interpretations of the book of Job, some of these interpreters have suggested that perhaps there is a way to affirm the differing voices without marginalization. True dialogue, as Bakhtin explains, is "unfinalizable," and in the case of Job has been going on for millennia.[15]

---

15. Two other examples that explore the possibility that the disputatious character of the book of Job is a metaphor for how we can approach the book itself are in Adams, "Goodness of Job's Bad Arguments"; and Alissa Jones Nelson, "Justice and Biblical Interpretation." In the former, Adams sees Job as a part and parcel of the Old Testament itself, which presents differing views of God in dialogue with one another, and then pits Calvin, Barth, and Aquinas against each other to arrive at a conclusion about the nature and utility of argument. Jones Nelson uses the contrapuntal theories of Edward Said to test two differing liberationist readings of Job for their value.

Meaning in Individual Passages

Job 19:25–27 ("For I know that my Redeemer lives,
  and that at the last he will stand upon the earth;
and after my skin has been thus destroyed,
  then in my flesh I shall see God,
whom I shall see on my side,
  and my eyes shall behold, and not another.
  My heart faints within me!")

Within the debate itself are several profound statements, some of which have proven more important than others in assessments of Job. The most widely quoted passage from all of the book of Job is certainly 19:25, which choirs around the world sing every Christmas and Easter in the context of Jesus's incarnation and resurrection. Within the book of Job, the passage falls in the context of the court case that Job brings to his tormentor—God (19:7–12). The problem he finds himself in is that no one—not his friends, his relatives, or his wife—takes his side (19:13–20). Because everyone seems to be against him, though he remains certain that he is in the right, Job claims that he will eventually be redeemed. The question is how his redemption will work since the climax of the chapter is notoriously difficult to interpret.

In 19:23, Job wishes that his legal case were recorded in stone, presumably so that people would not forget the case after he dies and is no longer able to plead his own case. Despite his earlier desire to have never been born due to his misery, Job has progressed throughout the argument to show a semblance of hope that he will be proven right in the end, even if he is not there to appreciate his redemption. With his hope in mind, he makes his famous claim—that he knows that his redeemer (*gō'ēl*) lives and will stand upon the earth. Many have wondered as to the identity of this redeemer. The NRSV capitalizes the first letter, indicating that its editors identify the redeemer as God, a common belief. In verse 26, after all, Job expects to see God in his own flesh. Also, if one reads the passage in hindsight after having read the book as a whole, Job perhaps foreshadows his eventual redemption where God declares that Job did speak right (42:7) after Job sees him with his eyes (42:5). There is a tension in the book of Job between the God he experiences and the God in whom he has faith. In 42:5, Job confirms that his understanding of the God he experiences was thankfully mistaken. He had heard of God, but now that he sees God, he can reject the hypothetical God who was his enemy and can accept the God he hoped would be his witness (16:19) and redeemer (19:25).[16]

Nevertheless, others claim it is difficult to understand how Job could expect God to take his side against God in the context of chapter 19.[17] As I mentioned above, Job's argument with his friends assumes that the system of retributive theology has been violated. It seems unlikely that Job would instill the violator of that system to stand up for him in court against himself. Job utters similarly in an earlier passage, where he says, "Surely now my witness is in heaven; He who can testify for me is on high . . . Let Him arbitrate between a man and God as between a man and his fellow. For a few more years will pass, and I shall

---

16. For two competing translations of the same passage in the same volume that nevertheless argue for a similar interpretation of 19:25, see Michel, "Confidence and Despair"; and Holman, "Does My Redeemer Live?" Holman writes that proponents of a third-party *gō'ēl* "seem to agree in their presupposition that the book of Job presents a static God who is '*Semper Idem*' and acts according to our laws of logic. But I rather follow those who maintain we have to distinguish between the traditional picture of God as presented by the three friends and the God Job wants to believe in the God of Ps 140,13"; Holman, "Does My Redeemer Live?" 378.

17. See especially Habel, *Book of Job*, 302–9.

Meaning in Individual Passages

go the way of no return." (16:19, 20–22 TNK) The editors of the Tanakh, like the editors of the NRSV in chapter 19, capitalize "him," indicating they believe Job expects God to arbitrate between Job and God. Many recent commentators, however, believe that Job has in mind a third party who will be his witness in chapter 16 and his redeemer in chapter 19. One other reason to accept a third party, other than the logic stated above, comes from the precedent set in the prologue. *Hassatan* acts as a prosecutor in the heavenly court, so it does not stand outside of reason to expect another celestial witness to stand up as defender for Job. Job, it would seem, would have no other choice than to desire a third party to defend him against the one who is laying siege against him (19:12).

One could say more about the right way of interpreting the passage in question, but that would still not fully explain how 19:25–27 has become a lens through which many interpret the book of Job as a whole. The answer, of course, lies in why the passage is so famous, which could also serve to solve the logical fallacy described above—how Job could possibly want God to defend him against God. In Handel's *Messiah* Job does not make an appearance. Rather a soprano soloist appropriates Job's words ("I know that my redeemer lives") to describe the resurrection of Jesus, the world's redeemer. Handel was not the first to find Jesus in Job's words. In fact, Jerome writes of 19:25 that Job "hopes for a resurrection; nay, rather he knew and saw that Christ, his redeemer, was alive, and at that last day would rise again from the earth." Gregory the Great's *Moralia*, a commentary that contains reams of allegorical interpretation on the book of Job, finds Jesus in even his literal interpretation of 19:25, writing, "For he who does not say, 'Creator,' but 'Redeemer,' expressly tells of Him, Who after He created all things, appeared Incarnate amongst us, that He might redeem us from a state of bondage, and by His Passion set us free from death everlasting."[18]

A christological interpretation of 19:25–27 thereby maintains both interpretive possibilities for the identity of the *gō'ēl*. Jesus as *gō'ēl* is both a third party advocating on behalf of humanity and also one with God. It should go without saying, of course, that as satisfying a christological interpretation of the *gō'ēl* might be for some, it does not work in a Jewish context, whether in the pre-Christian, Persian era that produced the book of Job or in the modern era where Jews find as much meaning in the book as Christians.

Nevertheless, it can be very difficult for some to resist the temptation to find Christ in the book of Job. Even Thomas Aquinas, who set out to write a commentary on Job that intentionally did not replicate the allegorical interpretation of Gregory the Great before him, concluded that Job spoke right in his belief in the resurrection of the dead and that his friends denied the resurrection, and thus spoke wrong. Job's words at the end of chapter 19, that after his skin has been destroyed he will still see God with his own eyes and in his flesh, bears witness to Job's belief in the resurrection. In this way, Job does not prefigure Jesus explicitly but anticipates the promise that Jesus's resurrection foretells.

Job 28 (The Poem on Wisdom)

The book of Job is often placed in the category or genre of wisdom literature, which also includes the biblical books of Proverbs, Ecclesiastes, and several psalms (e.g. 1, 37, 119, and others). We can also find some examples of wisdom literature in the deuterocanon (apocrypha), such as the Wisdom of Solomon and Sirach, as well as extratestamental

18. Gregory I, *Morals*, xiv.67.

Meaning in Individual Passages

books and cognate texts from neighboring cultures, such as Egypt and Mesopotamia. One normally designates texts as wisdom literature by observing their use of language. Wisdom texts tend to draw from a common vocabulary (e.g. "wisdom," "understanding," "council") that, though not absent in texts from other genres, is relatively less common among the prophets, in the law, and in historical narrative. Likewise, though the prophets, law, and characters in narratives *occasionally* utilize the capability to observe the natural world as method for achieving wisdom, the wisdom texts use observation as a primary tool for understanding how God works in the world. Thematically, wisdom texts do not share the interest of the other canonical material in Israel's history and tend toward universal themes. Consider, for instance, that the character Job himself is not an Israelite, and that the book of Job is bereft of any details about Israel, Judah, or the exile.

The book of Proverbs, as its title suggests, turns real-world observations into pithy proverbs that generally reflect a poetic parallelism. The form of the proverb can also be observed in Ecclesiastes, Job, and the wisdom psalms, but readers have often recognized striking differences between Ecclesiastes and Job on the one hand and Proverbs on the other. In fact, Job and Ecclesiastes are often considered antiwisdom literature since they question the confidence that the sages of the Proverbs appear to have.[19]

---

19. Note, for instance, how similar some of Job's friends' comments are to Proverbs (i.e. Job 5:2–7). Consider also that the general thrust of much of Proverbs is that good behavior leads to rewards and that wickedness leads to destruction. Job, on the other hand, seems to want to demonstrate that the good behavior of Job leads to his destruction. Joel S. Kaminsky is right, however, to point out the problems with generalizing both Proverbs and Job in this simplistic way (Kaminsky, "Would You Impugn My Justice?" 299–310). For one, he shows that the so-called retributive theology of the Proverbs

Whether one wants to categorize Job as wisdom or antiwisdom, the subject of wisdom is important in the book of Job. Tremper Longman, in fact, argues that the central question of the book of Job is "What is the source of wisdom?"[20] Strangely, Longman does not place much importance on chapter 28, which falls in the center of one of the outlines of the book of Job posited above. After all, chapter 28 of Job asks explicitly where wisdom comes from (28:20). Unfortunately, there is little consensus as to basic issues regarding chapter 28, which has made interpreting the chapter with much confidence somewhat difficult. For instance, who is speaking the words in chapter 28? Because there is no heading introducing the words, and because chapter 29 opens with a heading that suggests that Job had stopped speaking, most scholars have concluded that some narrator outside the narrative of the book speaks the words of chapter 28. The poem on wisdom, therefore, is an interlude in the general narrative of Job. If this is the case, the purpose of Job 28 seems to be to aid readers in their interpretation of the rest of the narrative.[21]

Another interpretation of the hymn to wisdom is that it continues the speech of Job from chapter 27. Even though chapter 29 says that "Job again took up his discourse," chapter 28 gives us no other reason to think that Job stops speaking for the sake of someone else. Even if chapter 28 were to come out of the mouth of a narrator, the characters in the plot would have no reason to think that Job ceased speaking in order for him to "again take up his discourse" in chapter 29. In other words, they do not acknowledge that

---

and the Psalms is more nuanced than generally perceived. Secondly, he demonstrates that Job's friends' speeches begin as quite nuanced and less rigid than most people tend to perceive them to be.

20. Longman, *Job*, 52.

21. See Newsom, *Book of Job*, 169–81.

Meaning in Individual Passages

someone else speaks, and so to the characters there is no break in Job's speech.

As far as the plausibility that the character Job would voice the poem of chapter 28, we can find a comparison between it and Job's first speech in chapter 3, where Job speaks out loud with no obvious addressee.[22] Job's temper has obviously eased since chapter 3, but in both speeches, he expresses a sentiment of futility. In his first speech, Job decides that his life would have been better had he never been born, and in chapter 28, Job decides that a human is not capable of finding wisdom. Thus, both Jan Fokkelman and Alison Lo see chapter 28 as the final speech of the dialogue, which effectively acts as an inclusio with chapter 3[23] on the one hand and a bridge to Job's final defense on the other.

If one were to view Job as the speaker of chapter 28, she would see Job reflecting abstractly on his experience up to this point and end that reflection with a statement that leads to his final defense. He begins by comparing wisdom to rare metals or gems that must be mined from deep in the earth, but unlike those metals, wisdom remains hidden and buried (28:1–11). Animals that roam the earth where humans do not go also do not see wisdom (28:7–8). Next, Job notes that one cannot take the jewels and metals one can retrieve from mines and buy wisdom in the marketplace (28:12–19). Job in his current state has lost all his wealth that would have given him leverage in the market, but that would not have provided him with wisdom. For there is no way for a human to find wisdom. It is beyond our capability, even after death (28:20–22). Only God has access to wisdom since God established the earth with wisdom (28:23–27). Job then finishes with a proverb, perhaps a realization

22. Fokkelman, *Book of Job in Form*, 269.
23. Ibid., 269; Lo, *Job 28 as Rhetoric*, 197.

that leads to his final defense: "And he said to humankind, 'Truly, the fear of the Lord is wisdom, and to depart from evil is understanding'" (28:28). Because humanity has no ability to find wisdom on its own, the individual must get to wisdom through the god who established the earth with wisdom.

In this reflection of wisdom, the readers are brought back to the beginning of the book of Job and even the divine wager, where *hassatan* observes that Job has acted morally because of the protections afforded him by God. Those protections include wealth, which is reflected in property such as land, livestock, and servants. The melding of these characterizations of Job—piety and wealth—demands a deeper understanding of what it means to be a servant of God by that servant himself. Job, therefore, comes to the realization and follows that with a list of all the things that should have brought him wisdom—all those things in his life that show that he did fear the Lord and turned away from evil.[24]

This reading of chapter 28 is not without its own problems. Clines recognizes the awkwardness in attributing the poem to an unnamed narrator but also cannot square Job as the speaker of the poem. He therefore argues that the poem has been misplaced in chapter 28 and should be the conclusion of Elihu's speech.[25] We will look more closely at

24. See, for instance, Janzen, *Job*, 188; and Fokkelman, *Book of Job in Form*, 209.

25. Clines first argues that the poem on wisdom fits better with Elihu's speech and then hypothesizes how a page of text (chapters 28–31) in an early manuscript could have been sewn in the wrong place, changing all subsequent versions of Job. In the original version of Job, chapters 28–31 would have come after Elihu's speech, which would have come just after a full third cycle of debate. Chapter 28 would complete Elihu's speech, and Job's final defense would follow (Clines, "Putting Elihu in His Place," 243–53; see also, Clines, *Job 21–37*, 909). To my knowledge, no other major commentator has accepted this proposed reconstruction.

Meaning in Individual Passages

Elihu and how chapter 28 might complement his words in a few pages. Now, we will just point out that Clines argues that the fear of the Lord and turning from evil "proved to be [Job's] undoing" in the first chapter, so it seems unlikely that Job would perceive such behavior to be how one accesses wisdom.

Job 32–37 (Elihu's Speeches)

As I mentioned in the previous chapter, the case of Elihu is particularly complicated, due largely to the lack of consensus as to that material's date and provenance with respect to the rest of the book of Job. Many, if not most, interpreters and commentators in the modern era have considered Elihu a later addition to the book. Of those who consider Elihu late, many view the additions as contributing little to the book as a whole,[26] while others see a fresher point of view to the dialogues, but only by degrees.[27]

The purpose in this section is not to relitigate Elihu's place in the book of Job but to explore what it would mean for the book to be interpreted if we were to assume Elihu's speeches to be original to the text. To be sure, Elihu has

---

26. Consider Karl Barth, who writes, "Whatever view we take of the interposition of the speeches of Elihu, we must agree that they themselves do not accomplish nor even prepare the way for [resolving Job's ordeal]." Barth, *CD* IV.3.1, 422.

27. Cf. Newsom, *Book of Job*, 207, who sees Elihu's speeches as "reframing . . . what counts as relevant" to create a "moral imagination that is in significant ways different from that of the friends." However, Elihu remains a bit of an outsider in her estimation since his speeches were added in the late Persian to early Hellenistic era. Thus, Elihu was not original to the plot, which does not matter in her evaluation of the book of Job as a "contest of moral imaginations" but would disrupt other readings of the book of Job that view Elihu as offering one of two divine responses to Job, which we entertain in this section.

not always held such a dismissed position among Job interpreters. In John Calvin's many sermons on the book of Job, Elihu comes across as the true hero of the book, indeed, the "mouthpiece of God."[28] Medieval Jewish commentators, particularly Saadiah Gaon and Maimonides, portray Elihu as the most convincing debater among the friends. After all, "Job did not offer rebuttal to him but held his peace."[29]

The conclusions of the premodern readers concerning Elihu are not surprising. If one presumes the integrity of the Masoretic Text, the Vulgate, and the Septuagint, the absence of any discussion of Elihu by the other characters or God in the story would cause no problem. More importantly, God does not challenge Elihu as God challenges Job throughout chapters 38–41. Nor does God condemn Elihu's words as God does to "Eliphaz . . . and [his] two friends" (42:7). Of course, modern critics understandably find the absence of mention of Elihu as evidence of his speeches being a later addition. That is, the reason Elihu is not challenged or condemned by God is that Elihu was not present for the speeches or the verdict. Rather, some other writer than he or she who wrote the bulk of Job added Elihu at a later date.

As I mentioned in the previous chapter, however, recent critics have begun to treat Elihu as integral to the book of Job, viewing him much as Calvin, Saadiah and Maimonides did. C. L. Seow has emerged as one of Elihu's biggest champions, positing Elihu as not merely a wise fourth friend whose words are not rebuked but actually as a conduit for God in the same tradition as some celebrated prophets of the Hebrew Bible. Consider first his name, which could be translated as "he is my God." The inclusion in his name of the name for God, *'ēl*, is something that Elihu shares with

---

28. Schreiner, *Where Shall Wisdom Be Found?*, 131–35.
29. Sa'adia, *Book of Theodicy*, 348.

Meaning in Individual Passages

Daniel, Ezekiel, Samuel, and Elijah.[30] Like these other figures, Elihu mediates God's revelation by way of dreams, visions, or God's spirit (32:8) and promotes mediation of this sort as God's preferred method of communication (33:14, 15). Elihu himself is not divine, nor does he represent as profound a revelation as the *mal'ak YHWH* (the "angel of the Lord"). Rather, he is a flawed human who speaks the word of God. He "bring[s his] knowledge from far away and ascribe[s] righteousness to [his] Maker" (36:3). Elihu offers Job "perfect knowledge" as God's conduit (36:4).[31]

If, then, we take Elihu at his word—that he speaks the word of God as response to Job—what is the answer that Job has been seeking? Elihu reassures Job that he is human like Job (33:6), and thus Job should not fear him. Job will wait until he needs to gird up his loins in the presence of the deity (38:3). And so Elihu offers some ways that God does speak to his people by way of possible explanation of how God works in the world, such as bringing about suffering as a way of instruction (33:19) and allowing for an angelic intercessor who might pray (33:23) so that the sufferer might be "redeemed from going down to the Pit" and that he or she will "see the light" (33:28). Thus, Job's conclusions, based on the retributive theology of his friends—that God has found fault in Job despite Job's piety—misunderstands how God works in the world (33:8–11). God is not limited to a single doctrine of retributive theology, but is free to work in the world as a God beyond any system.

30. Seow, "Elihu's Revelation," 268–69. Seow calls these names Elistic, which invokes the name of the deity called El (of Canaanite origin, originally) as opposed to referring to Yahweh, whose name has its origins in Ugarit. By the time of the writing of the book of Job, the two names were considered different names for the same Israelite deity, but the Elistic tradition remained as distinct from Yahwistic traditions.

31. See also 32:8, 9, 18; and 33:1–4.

Elihu peppers his speech with quotes from throughout the dialogues (inspiring another charge against his being an original character in the story, since he is the only character that explicitly quotes others), including the forensic language from Job's lawsuit, such as "justice" and "lawsuit." The problem with a trial, Elihu posits, is that God is not bound by the same systems of justice as Job and his friends are assuming. God's transcendence, Elihu argues, means that God is not affected by sin in the same way as humanity (35:6–8) and so cannot be brought to trial in the same way as a human can.

Thus, Elihu responds to the stalemate argument of Job and his friends. The chiastic structure of the book of Job makes this clear. Yahweh's unmediated revelation following Elihu (38–41) should satisfy Job's desire to speak to God directly, but its main concern is Job's first speech (chapter 3), wherein Job assaults creation with his myopic death wish. Elihu, on the other hand, answers the questions raised throughout the dialogue itself. The friends irritate him with their inability to answer Job satisfactorily. Elihu, repeating the word "answer" (*'nh*) nine times in his dialogue, offers the intellectual "answer" to the problem and prepares the way for the transcendent response of Yahweh from the tempest.[32]

Job 38–41 (The Voice from the Tempest)

After thirty-seven chapters wherein God makes a wager with Satan and remains silent throughout Job's sufferings and arguments, readers, along with Job, are certainly ready

32. Seow, "Elihu's Revelation," 264. Maimonides, *Guide of the Perplexed*, 462, notes several passages in Elihu's speech that anticipate the voice from the tempest, such as his referencing natural phenomena as a form of revelation and distinguishing himself further from the three friends.

Meaning in Individual Passages

to see how God will finally respond to Job's complaints and his friends' theological claims. God's response is puzzling, to say the least—some would even say troubling. The voice from the tempest, rather than comforting Job in his suffering, seems to berate him for asking questions in the first place, sarcastically positing questions of his own that chide Job on his insignificance.

> Who is this that darkens counsel by words without knowledge?
> Gird up your loins like a man,
> I will question you,
> and you shall declare to me.
> Where were you when I laid the foundation of the earth? Tell me, if you have understanding.
> Who determined its measurements—surely you know!
> Or who stretched the line upon it? (38:2–5)

And the questions keep coming for the entirety of God's response.

Somehow the litany of rhetorical questions satisfies Job. Perhaps, as Elie Wiesel argues, Job pretends to be satisfied to get God to stop tormenting him in this new way.[33] Or, perhaps God genuinely answers Job's concerns. Job consistently asks for an encounter with God, and in his final words declares his intent to confront God (31:37). Perhaps God's revelation alone satisfies Job enough since Job is one of the very few biblical characters who can claim to have seen God face to face.[34] No doubt because it is God who answers Job and does so near the end of the book, most

---

33. "By repenting sins he did not commit, by justifying a sorrow he did not deserve, he communicates to us that he did not believe in his own confessions; they were nothing but decoys" (Wiesel, "Job: Our Contemporary," 235).

34. Habel, *Book of Job*, 536.

readers assume that the true meaning of the book of Job is to be found in these words.

Being that as it may, the questions on the surface have little to do with any of Job's specific sufferings or anything Job or his friends mention. After the opening lines (38:2–3), God discusses cosmogony (38:4–21), meteorology (38:22–38), zoology (38:39—39:30), and finishes with lengthy discussions on the characters of Behemoth and Leviathan, which may either be mythical creatures or the hippopotamus and crocodile respectively (40:15—41:34).[35] What, if anything, do these subjects have to do with losing one's family and property to marauding raiders, losing one's health to a skin disease, and losing one's friends through argument?

Because the voice from the tempest comes at the end of the story, and because the voice is God's, chapters 38–41 have attracted the most attention from interpreters eager to unlock the meaning of the book of Job. This is the moment we have all been waiting for, and it unfortunately takes work to figure out. If, however, God gave a pat answer to Job's problems, the book of Job would likely not have maintained its place in the imagination of so many people over such a long time. Though there is much agreement over the importance of the divine speeches, there is a surprisingly diverse array of interpretations. A detailed survey of the various interpretations of this one speech would be its own book, but some interpretations are more compelling than others, and these usually focus on how the text of Yahweh's speech alludes to other passages in the earlier sections of

---

35. Whether the Leviathan is the crocodile or another mythical creature is up for debate and may make little difference. Job's first readers may not have recognized the difference between a crocodile and a Leviathan, considering they almost certainly had never seen a crocodile.

Meaning in Individual Passages

the book. Two readings I want to highlight not only stem from textual allusions but can also be supported by the two structural outlines detailed above (chapter 2).

If the interpreter views the structure of Job linearly, the movement of the dialogues leads to Job's final defense (29–31). In this way, the dialogue between Job and his friends is not a red herring that gets brushed aside by Yahweh until 42:7–8. Instead, the heated exchange progresses Job's thoughts. Job develops a thesis through the refining fire of debate and culminates in a closing statement that demands response from God. Job completes his final defense, challenging God to respond:

> O that I had one to hear me!
>> (Here is my signature! Let the Almighty answer me!)
>> O that I had the indictment written by my adversary!
>
> Surely I would carry it on my shoulder;
>> I would bind it on me like a crown;
>
> I would give him an account of all my steps;
>> like a prince I would approach him.
>> (31:35–37)

The Almighty, in fact, does answer Job, and Job keeps his word. Though the voice from the whirlwind does not refer directly to Job's words, Job, in his responses, alludes to his own earlier speeches. In 29:9–10, Job describes the honor he received "in [his] prime, / when the friendship of God was upon [his] tent" (29:4). "The nobles refrained from talking, / and laid their hands on their mouths"; he says, "the voices of princes were hushed, / and their tongues stuck to the roof of their mouths." When God responds to him, Job acts the same way to the one he honors by laying his hand upon his own mouth (40:4), and his final reply (in 42:6, which we will discuss in detail below) repeats the phrase "dust and ashes" that he uses to describe his situation in 30:19.³⁶ But this is not the only way to view God's response to Job.

If one sees the structure of Job as chiastic, as the second outline in chapter 2 demonstrates, the voice from the whirlwind acts as a response to Job's first speech in 3:1–26. Yahweh's opening lines in 38:2, which sets the stage for the rest of the poem, support this thesis. "Who is this that darkens (*maḥšiḵ*) council (*ʿeṣah*), by words (*millin*) without knowledge (*daʿat*)?" Yahweh asks. The Hebrew words *ʿeṣah* and *daʿat* are common in wisdom literature of the Hebrew Bible. The word *ʿeṣah* most generally means council, as it is most often translated in English Bibles. But it can also mean "plan" or "design," which is the likely intended meaning here. Throughout the dialogues, Job has been describing the breakdown of a system. The voice from the tempest refutes that charge. The system (what is often called retributive theology) has not broken down, because that system is not a valid description of how the world works in the first place. There is a plan, as 38:2 suggests, but Job has no knowledge of it. God will address the ignorance of Job's friends in the epilogue, but Job receives the longer, poetic response, not merely because of his ignorance, but because he has "darkened" the plan.

Yahweh accuses Job (though some have suggested that Elihu is the subject of 38:2) of darkening (*maḥšiḵ* with the root *ḥ-š-k*) God's plans, alluding to Job's opening line in chapter 3: "Let the day perish in which I was born, and the night that said, 'A man-child (*geḇer*) is conceived.' Let

---

36. Newsom, *Book of Job*, 238. The weakness of this view lies in the intrusion of Elihu, who may be a later addition to the book of Job, making the flow of the book a victim of historical development. Or, one could have a more positive view where Elihu adds dramatic suspense for a more satisfying climax.

Meaning in Individual Passages

that day be darkness [*ḥošek* from the root *ḥ-š-k*]! May God above not seek it, or light shine on it." Job's particular death-wish requires the killing of the light on that day, reversing the language God uses on the first day in Gen 1:3. Job 3:4 literally begins, "That day, let it be darkness." Yahweh's response is to restore the light by redescribing the creation of the cosmos through his rhetorical questions—re-creation by divine fiat.[37]

Alter notes several other words and ideas that Yahweh pulls from Job's first speech, turning "Job's first affirmation of death into an affirmation of life."[38] Job calls himself a "man-child" (*geber*) on the night he was born, and so Yahweh tells him to "gird up [his] loins like a man (*geber*)" in 38:3, preparing Job for a rude awakening. In 38:19–20, Yahweh reestablishes the light (*'ôr*) that Job wanted to extinguish (3:4–6). Other words or ideas Yahweh reappropriates from Job's first speech include "womb" (38:8//3:10); "hedge" (38:8//3:23); and "morning stars" (38:7//3:9). Thus, the evidence that Yahweh responds to Job's first speech seems to outweigh any other theses.[39]

Even so, the majority of Yahweh's response from the tempest deals with zoology, which does not seem to have anything to do with Job's speech or with any of the rest of the book of Job other than the livestock Job loses early in chapter 1. The surprise change in subject matter affects a vision of the book itself. Job's opening gambit darkens God's

37. Alter, *Biblical Poetry*, 95–110, offers a convincing and detailed argument for this thesis.

38. Ibid., 97.

39. There may be room here for a comic interpretation of the text, where Yahweh is responding to Job's first speech in chapter 3, but Job, by virtue of his using words from his final defense to respond to Yahweh, understands Yahweh as responding to his concluding statements. Thus, the book ends in confusion, which may seem appropriate to some.

plans because it portrays a myopic vision of the world. The friends are wrong because they sustain the solipsistic worldview that Job imagines but interpret it differently. But according to Yahweh, the world is not about Job and what he does.

In chapter 28, the speaker of the poem on wisdom portrays wisdom as essentially ungraspable but for the fearing of the Lord. When the Lord finally speaks, Job receives another vision of the wisdom of God. To the human the world may seem chaotic—the world where the weather can often threaten one's life in one instance (38:22–25) or relieve an unpopulated wasteland in another (38:26); where some animals threaten the existence of others (38:39) and other animals seem so foolish that they fly (or do not fly, in the case of the ostrich) in the face of any human understanding of wisdom (39:13–18). The Lord's response, therefore, is not intended to answer Job's questions but to reframe Job's understanding of the way the world works.

Jean Lévêque proposes that through the speeches from the tempest Yahweh argues that the vastness of the world and the freedom of the animals in it point to the limitation of humanity with respect to the duration of life, knowledge, and power. The freedom of the animals, though, should not frighten Job so much as enliven in him a capacity for wonder. The brutality of the world, therefore, should not be something to blame God for, as Job does earlier in the book, but rather it works as a vehicle for correcting an anthropocentric myopia. The wide assortment of animals that challenge humanity's reign over the earth, therefore, corrects Job's understanding of how the world works, especially regarding God's providence.[40]

But why so many animals? In 40:3–5, perhaps browbeaten by chapters 38 and 39, Job places his hand on his

---

40. Lévêque, "L'interprétation des discours de YHWH," 217.

Meaning in Individual Passages

mouth and says he will add no more to his complaint. Yet Yahweh continues his inventory of the wildest of his creations. The most significant of these is the last—Leviathan—for its identity is not entirely clear. As I suggested above, Leviathan could simply be a crocodile as described by a poet who may or may not have actually seen a real crocodile. The poet of Job likely relied primarily on others' descriptions and his own imagination to conjure up an image of a crocodile from a faraway land.

On the other hand, Leviathan is the only creature, animal or otherwise, not explicitly described as a creation of Yahweh in the speech from the tempest.[41] Perhaps Leviathan represents something altogether different. Elsewhere in the Hebrew Bible and in extrabiblical texts from the ancient southwest Asia, Leviathan is a supernatural creature representing evil.[42]

Like the rest of the speech from the tempest, Yahweh's mention of Leviathan alludes to specific aspects of Job's speech in chapter 3. Note, however, that unlike the stars or God's creation, Leviathan is not collateral damage stemming from Job's curse, but a tool of the curse itself (3:8). Job is not vanquishing Leviathan along with the stars that bring light to the day of his birth, but calling on Leviathan to do the vanquishing. Thus, Yahweh is not re-creating Leviathan after Job has called for the destruction of his day. Rather, Yahweh is acknowledging the existence of evil in the world through the metaphor of a supernatural being that ancient readers would recognize as a competing force. However, this competing force is no more a threat than one of Yahweh's other creations.

---

41. Levenson, *Creation and the Persistence of Evil*, 49.

42. For a more thorough examination of Leviathan, see Caquot, "Le Léviathan de Job 40:25—41:26"; and Ortlund, "Identity of Leviathan," 17–30.

Reading Leviathan this way, as a supernatural being representing evil, suggests that Yahweh is tacitly explaining Job's source of suffering.[43] Critics of Job often complain that the voice from the tempest could not satisfy Job's complaints since it ignores Job's suffering altogether. This reading perceives Yahweh as the only one who can suppress the evil that Leviathan wreaks.

This thesis about Leviathan is not watertight though. First, rather than comforting Job by reining in Leviathan, Yahweh seems to be warning Job not to arouse Leviathan (which Job attempts to do in 3:8); only Yahweh is able to contain Leviathan's destructive activity. Also, if we are to see Elihu as the one who responds to the mistaken theology of Job's friends, then this supernatural explanation of evil is unnecessary. After all, in the end, Job's concern is with God's absence. God satisfies Job because of the theophany more than content of the speech. The content of the speech corrects Job's first speech, which Job seems to acknowledge in 42:1–6, as we will see below.

Job 42:1–6 (Job's Response)

How then, does Job respond to such an enigmatic revelation? Modern readers often seem disappointed or confused. How does the speech from the tempest properly respond to such suffering as Job has experienced? Job learns nothing of the wager with *hassatan* and is given no real answer as to why he had to undergo such loss. In the context of the narrative, though, the one thing we can say about Job's response is that he is satisfied. Something in God's revelation answered Job's pleading. What is less clear, though, is in what way Job's satisfaction manifests itself. This is due to a very ambiguous verse, which also happens to be the

---

43. Ortlund, "Identity of Leviathan," 28–29.

Meaning in Individual Passages

last thing out of Job's mouth in the book. The NRSV translates 42:6 as "Therefore I despise myself, and repent in dust and ashes," which is a typical translation of the Masoretic Text, roughly equivalent to other English translations (ESV, NIV, KJV) as well as most translations in other languages including the Latin Vulgate and the Septuagint (which has Job consider himself dust and ashes rather than repent in them). These multiple translations are likely the result of inertia, for they promote a common reading of a text that is anything but obvious.

The passage begins clearly enough. After Yahweh completes the discourse on Leviathan, Job responds with general agreement to the overall message from the tempest. Job knows that God can do all things and that Job, himself, has spoken what he did not understand until now. Job's main point in the early verses is to contrast his limited knowledge with God's vast knowledge, which seems to have been the point of the speech from the tempest.[44] Job says in 42:5, "I have heard of you by the hearing of the ear, but now my eye sees you," signifying that Job's previous experience with God was secondhand. His current experience, by contrast, is face-to-face, as Abraham and Moses had experienced.

This seeing with the eye is certainly at the heart of Job's satisfaction. God's speech is an important correction of Job's opening gambit in chapter 3, but God's mere appearance in the tempest seems more important to Job in his current state, because Job's declaration of the theophany in 42:5 leads to Job's final words in 42:6.

Before positing what I believe are more plausible interpretations of 42:6, let us explore the implications of the translations offered in the NRSV et al. Job's speech in 42:1–5 implies that things with him have changed. He now understands things he did not before or, at the very

44. Wolde, "Job 42:1–6," 231.

least, recognizes that there are things he cannot understand. He thus implies that he has been chastened and has relinquished his previous position. Strangely, though, 42:6 suggests that very little has changed for Job. In chapter 3, Job expresses his wish that he had never been born, certainly expressing that he detests his life. In 9:21, Job uses the exact word (*m's*) to describe how he views himself ("I loathe my life" with "my life" an obvious object of the sentence). In 19:18, Job claims that young children despise (*m's*) him, which is typical of much of Job's wallowing in pity throughout the dialogues. Elihu, on the other hand, uses the same verb to describe God in 36:5: "Surely God is mighty and he does not despise (*m's*) [anyone]." For Job to say that after his recognition of God's speech he "therefore" despises himself seems to ignore all his previous despising himself. The "therefore" implies something has changed because of what immediately precedes his despising. Intellectually, things *have* changed for him—he has changed his mind about how God works in the world—but his opinion of himself remains one of pity.

As for the second half of 36:5, nothing much changes here either, other than his repentance, if that is how we choose to interpret the verb *nḥm*. In 2:8 Job sits in ashes, and in 2:12 his friends throw dust on their heads. In 30:19, Job declares that he has "become like dust and ashes": that is, he has one foot in the grave. In 42:6, Job certainly says something about dust and ashes, but immediately following 42:6 he is redeemed and is no longer sitting on dust and ashes. His period of mourning has obviously come to an end, making his final statement strangely muted in the context of the epilogue of the book.

In light of such a problematic interpretation of Job's final words, allow me to offer other equally grammatically plausible readings of 42:6 that are more consistent with what

Meaning in Individual Passages

we know about the rest of the book of Job. These alternative interpretations first recognize a problem with the verb *m's* ("reject"), in that the verse does not provide an object for Job to reject. Thus, a literal translation of 42:6 might be "Therefore I reject and repent upon dust and ashes." What, then, does Job reject? Most translations, as indicated above, make the verb reflexive, which is not justified by its usage elsewhere without reading it in a different stem (niphal instead of qal). Two potential objects other than "myself" exist in the rest of the text of 42:1–6. One object is before the verb, wherein Job retracts his words (or case against God) from earlier in the book. Thus, he says, "I reject [my preceding case against God] and repent upon/concerning[45] dust and ashes.[46] The other object would be the dust and ashes that act as the object of *nḥm* as well in 42:6: I reject and repent of/with respect to the dust and ashes.[47]

The second problem with the verse is the meaning of the verb *niḥamtî* with the preposition *'al*, which could mean any of the following based on precedent from other biblical texts using the same combination of words: "I have changed my mind about dust and ashes,"[48] "I am sorry upon dust and ashes,"[49] "I am consoled about dust and ashes,"[50] or "I have completed the rites of mourning upon dust and ashes."[51]

---

45. We will reconsider the meaning of the preposition *'al* in the context presently.

46. Kuyper, "Repentance of Job"; Habel, *Book of Job*, 576; Fokkelman, *Book of Job in Form*, 317–19.

47. Patrick, "Translation of Job XLII 6"; Timmer, "God's Speeches, Job's Responses," 300.

48. See Exod 32:12.

49. See Judg 21:6.

50. See 2 Sam 13:39.

51. See Jer 31:15.

APPROACHING JOB

To determine what Job might mean in this, his final spoken verse, we must again look at the context of these words in the rest of the story. As indicated earlier in this section and as supported by the chiastic structure of the book of Job, Job begins the book with ten children, much livestock, and in good health. The book will end with Job having ten children, much livestock, and a life lived into old age. In between, however, Job suffers greatly and spends that time on ashes (2:8), arguing with friends who have come to console (*nḥm*) Job (2:11) and to sprinkle dust on their heads (2:12), and identifying with dust and ashes (30:19), indicating his proximity to death. This trajectory—from health to dust and ashes to health—would support a reading that brings Job off of the dust and ashes, not further on it. Immediately following 42:6, Job is off the ash heap, vindicated by God, and praying for his friends. The court case is over, Job is no longer complaining against God or about his state. It is difficult to see how anything that follows 42:6 would support a Job who despises himself and repents on dust and ashes.

Perhaps there is an implicit lacuna between 42:6 and 42:7, where Job continues to mourn and pity himself and that satisfies God enough to praise his words so that Job might arise from his sorrowful state. However, based on the text itself and the context of the book as a whole, it is certainly justifiable to read 42:6 more along the lines of "Therefore I quit, and have completed the rites of mourning upon dust and ashes."[52]

---

52. Habel's translation is, admittedly, more appropriately poetic and pithy: "Therefore I retract/And repent of dust and ashes" (*Book of Job*, 575). See also Fokkelman, *Book of Job in Form*, 318, whose translation reads, "Therefore I quit/and am consoled about [my state of] dust and ashes." Note also the tenth-century commentary of Sa'adiah, which is translated from the Arabic as, "Therefore do I spurn what I once said and take my solace in dust and ashes," proving disruption

Meaning in Individual Passages

Based on the context, therefore, the best reading of Job's response to the speech from the tempest has Job acknowledging God's omnipotence and agreeing that he had spoken of things he did not understand. In 40:4, 5, the only other time Job responds directly to Yahweh's speech, Job points entirely to what he has said. "I lay my hand on my mouth," he says, "I have spoken once, and I will not answer; twice, but will proceed no further." In chapter 42, Job gets a second chance to reply and says much the same thing. This time, however, he does not merely stop speaking, but retracts his words. He is satisfied with the response from the tempest. He has had his face-to-face encounter with God. He has no need to remain in a state of mourning. The question now is how God will respond to the retraction.

Job 42:7, 8 (God's Condemnation of Job's Friends)

After Job retracts his court case and ends his period of mourning, God turns his attention to Job's friends. The NRSV translates Job 42:7 and 8 as

> After the Lord had spoken these words to Job, the Lord said to Eliphaz the Temanite: 'My wrath is kindled against you and against your two friends; for you have not spoken of me what is right, as my servant Job has.' Now therefore take seven bulls and seven rams, and go to my servant Job, and offer up for yourselves a burnt offering; and my servant Job shall pray for you, for I will accept his prayer not to deal with you according to your folly; for you have not spoken of me what is right, as my servant Job has done.'

However God feels about Job's complaints from chapters 3 to 31, by 42:7, Job is on God's good side. In fact,

---

in the inertia of a flawed translation. Sa'adiah, *Book of Theodicy*, 410.

God is now seemingly much angrier at Job's friends than God ever was with Job. In fact, God calls Job "my servant" and bestows upon him the responsibility of priest for the friends. So not only is God angry with the friends, God has retracted any ill will at Job, if ill will is what we can describe as the sarcastic rhetoric from chapters 38 to 41.

That leads us to ask the important questions: What does Job say that is right? and What do Job's friends say that is wrong? Anyone who reads the book of Job would notice his sustained complaints as borderline attacks on God. How could that be considered speaking rightly of God? Also, if what Job says is considered speaking what is right of God, what do the friends say that is not right? After all, all their energy is spent defending God against Job's accusations. Theirs might be bad theology, but does bad theology warrant condemnation by God and intercession by Job, who seems to have shared the same retributive theology until his experience convinced him of its bankruptcy?

Scholars have attempted to answer in several ways the question of how these characters have and have not spoken rightly of God. I will review five of these attempts, positing that the best explanation depends on a different but more obvious reading of the phrase *lōʾ dibbartem ʾēlay* as "you have not spoken *to* me."

One school of thought regarding God's speech to Eliphaz determines that because there is evidence elsewhere that the prose and poetry sections come from different sources, the editor has stitched the two sections together while also omitting portions of the prose section where the three friends say something obviously theologically specious while Job speaks rightly of God. The poetic sections, wherein Job sounds impatient, condemning God for his fate and even wishing for death through the destruction of his birthday, have replaced the original middle section of the folktale. Thus, the generic incongruousness of the prose and poetic sections are matched by an incongruity of context as well.

This reading has multiple problems, not the least of which is how dissatisfying it is to read such a profound and compelling book and not *really* know what happens. In addition to a general dissatisfaction, the theory of the different sources is purely conjecture. We do not know which of Job's words might have been held in such high regard other than the words extant in the text itself. As reviewed in the previous chapter, more and more scholars see the book of Job as the product of a single author, or, at the most, the product of two authors, the latter of which contributed only the words of Elihu. There must certainly be a more likely explanation.

Another theory regards Job as denying that sin is always punished with affliction and as holding fast to his innocence whereas his friends have a more rigid reading of affliction. Norman Habel writes: "Yahweh's answer announces that Job's bold assertions in the dialogue speeches were likewise free from blame in spite of some rather vitriolic moments (e.g., 16:9ff.). The blunt and forthright accusations of Job from the depths of his agony are closer to the truth than the conventional unquestioning pronouncements of the friends . . . Job's answers correspond with reality. They are devoid of dissembling and flattery, a trait against which Job warned the friends."[53] That is, the difference between the words of Job and those of his friends is a question of theological method: Job speaks the truth from his experience while his friends' words are based on tradition and cold reason.

Though there is much to commend here, and I do think that the friends' "dissembling and flattery" relates to

53. Habel, *Book of Job*, 583.

their condemnation, the friends have not experienced what Job has experienced. The real difference between Job's theology and that of his friends seems to arise because Job's theology has been deconstructed in light of Job's unique experience. Had Eliphaz or Bildad lost everything due to a singular wager in heaven, who is to say they would have reacted as Job had and that Job would not have maintained his own theology of retribution?

A third option points to Job's words in 42:6. There, as we saw above, Job retracts his words without knowledge, and the friends did not. It is that Job repented that makes Job right. Thus, Job agrees with God in the end.

The problem with this reading is that the friends *do* agree with God (at least the God of their tradition). In fact, they spend much of their time telling Job he is wrong about God. In other words, Job retracts the very words Job's friends tell him to retract before God ever appears in the tempest. Job may have spoken rightly in his retraction, but nothing explains how Job's friends spoke wrongly. Also, again, Job is given the opportunity to repent when God speaks directly to him while the friends never really get the opportunity to repent in the dialogues.

Fourth, Stanley Porter searches for these right words of Job in vain, never pinpointing what they might be, suggesting in the end that the search "for what words Job says that are commended by God must end in ambiguity."[54] There may be no way to know, and we should be satisfied with that ambiguity theologically since it matches the story well. That is, characters throughout the book of Job remain ignorant of what happens in the heavenly court, Job never finds out about the divine wager, so it is appropriate for us to remain ignorant of what Job says that is commendable.

---

54. Porter, "Message of the Book of Job," 291–304.

Meaning in Individual Passages

A fifth interpretation, and the one I suggest is the best, argues that it is not a question of what Job says concerning God that is right, for God says that Job spoke without knowledge, and Job agrees. Instead, we are asking the wrong question. We should not be looking for what Job says, but how he says it—not *about* whom Job speaks, but *to* whom Job speaks.

Throughout the dialogues, Job never fails to address God, while the friends *never* address God. In some ways, Job's ignorance is his knowledge because it leads him to ask God himself for the truth. Karl Barth does not argue for a more accurate translation of 42:7–8 but recognizes the disparity in the dialogues themselves. He writes that "when we turn to the speeches of the friends, they do, of course, have something of the liveliness which is not lacking in the atmosphere of the class-room, and they may have well-weighed and perspicuous things to say on the problem, but they do not derive from the problem." In contrast, "the real truth of god and man is valid when God and man are engaged in eye-to-eye and mouth-to-ear encounter." In other words Job's friends sure do sound like they're speaking rightly about God, but their posture is all wrong.

Importantly, such a reading is justified by the text itself. A very basic translation of the condemnation of the friends would be "You have not spoken *to* me what is right as my servant Job has."[55] Of course, prepositions are notoriously difficult to translate, so one must look at other examples of the same verb *dbr* used with the same preposition *'el* to see how that combination of words is used in other places.[56]

---

55. Note the similarly phrased "The Lord would *speak to* Moses face to face as one speaks to his friend" from Exod 33:11. Considering the similarities between Job and Moses as discussed above, Exod 33:11 points us in a direction to translate *dibber 'el* as "speak to."

56. There are, depending on how one counts, somewhere around

Again, Job's friends not only never speak *to* God, but they even attempt to keep Job from speaking to God and to just accept that Job deserves what he has gotten. David Burrell writes, "Job is commended in the end because he dared to address the creator-God; his interlocutors are castigated for purporting to speak knowingly about that One. Speaking *about* something veers toward explaining, while speaking *to* someone can engage both in a relationship of exchange open to yet other forms of understanding."[57]

Last, note the immediate context: The penalty for the friends' speaking *about* God or on behalf of God and not *to* God is that they will go to Job with sacrifices and Job will pray for them. Job is shown as the one who is able to communicate with God in contradistinction to his friends. Thus, the most likely meaning is the simplest, and the meaning of the phrase becomes the clearest of the possibilities because of its simplicity.

While there is always more to say about Job, the above should suffice as an entry into the most important and contentious passages in the book. The final chapter will summarize the theological and ethical consequences of the book of Job as a whole, keeping these individual passages in mind.

---

two hundred examples of *dbr 'el* in the Hebrew Bible, and of those two hundred examples, Isa 32:6 is unambiguously not "speak to" but either "to speak in error *concerning* the Lord" or "to preach disloyalty *against* the Lord." However, 99 percent of the time this combination of words means "speak to." Since the context of the book of Job as a whole justifies this reading, I think it is a plausible interpretation of the text, and one that we should entertain.

57. Burrell, *Deconstructing Theodicy*, 124.

Meaning in Individual Passages

REVIEW QUESTIONS

1. *Hassatan* asks, "Does Job serve God for nothing?" How would you answer that question?
2. At the end of the book, Yahweh says that Eliphaz and his friends did not speak what is right. What is the purpose of having Eliphaz and his friends say so much if what they say is wrong in the end?
3. How does the proposal that Yahweh charges Job's friends with not speaking right "*to* me" as opposed to "*about* me" affect how you answer question 2?
4. How is the book of Job considered wisdom literature?
5. What is Leviathan? What is Leviathan's function in the book of Job?

4

SOME THEOLOGICAL, PASTORAL, AND ETHICAL IMPLICATIONS OF THE BOOK OF JOB

IN A RECENT BOOK on Job, Harold Kushner writes, "If there is more interest in the book of Job today among people who are not regular students of the Bible, I think we can attribute that to two things: to cancer and to Adolf Hitler."[1] While there may be some truth to Kushner's theory, bad things have been happening to good people since well before Hitler or our knowledge of cancer, and people have been using Job as a way to understand suffering for a significant period of that time as well. I've tried to show the influence of Job throughout the centuries in this book, pulling interpreta-

1. Kushner, *Book of Job*, 165.

Some Theological, Pastoral, and Ethical Implications

tions of different parts of Job from Jewish and Christian writers from all different eras—ancient, medieval, Enlightenment, and modern.

Most of the work I have drawn from has been explicitly scholarly—by biblical scholars, theologians, or philosophers—but there are many other ways people have engaged with the book of Job. Novelists, playwrights, and filmmakers, especially, have used the book of Job to explore modern issues, usually to do with suffering of all kinds.

Voltaire wrote *Candide* as an Enlightenment update on the book of Job in response to the Lisbon earthquake of 1755. How could a good God allow suffering like that earthquake on such a scale? Søren Kierkegaard and Franz Kafka, in strikingly similar ways, use Job to explore failed romantic relationships in *Repetition* and *The Trial*, respectively. Archibald Macleish's play *J. B.* explores the emptiness of mid-twentieth-century life through a modern Job. Elie Wiesel's *The Trial of God* hints at the trial that Job brings in the dialogues to question the benevolence of God after the Holocaust.[2] Terence Malick's film *The Tree of Life* begs God to answer a family suffering after the death of a beloved family member, quoting the book of Job throughout. More recently, Andrey Zvyagintsev's film *Leviathan* points to the book of Job as a way of grappling with the tortuous bureaucracy and abuse of power in Vladimir Putin's Russia.

Even some of the more scholarly interpretations in the reception history of Job evidently stem from the writers' reflections on their personal experiences. Pope Gregory I, also known as Saint Gregory the Great, whose *Moralia in Job* stretches to more than a million words, likely was drawn to work on the book of Job because of a great illness

---

2. Wiesel's play is kind of a double-allegory since it views the ancient book of Job through the lens of a pogrom in 1649 in order to bear witness to the Holocaust.

he experienced. Immanuel Kant, who seems about as different from Gregory as one could be, identified with Job during his own life and used Job to illustrate a philosophical treatise, as we will see below.

How, then, does Job help this wide variety of writers? Does he even answer their questions on the meaning of their suffering, whether physical, social, spiritual, or psychic?

In this last brief chapter I will highlight some of the most important unifying theological themes that readers of the book of Job have seen: suffering, freedom, and creation.

SUFFERING AND THEODICY

As I noted above, personal suffering has drawn many people to the book of Job, either for answers to their suffering or commiseration with another sufferer. One can imagine how many people undergoing great pain would want to understand the reason for it. The book of Job, because of its premise and its placement in the biblical canon seems an obvious place for many to look. The fact that God responds to Job at the end is naturally a further draw. It would seem, then, that the book of Job must justify God's activity on earth, which is why one often sees the book of Job associated with the term *theodicy*, which comes from the Greek words *theos* ("god") and *dike* ("justice").[3]

What one finds after reading the book of Job, as we have seen, is that very little in the book satisfactorily answers the question of why bad things happen to good people. In fact, readers of the book of Job, however they were

---

3. Gottfried Leibniz coined the term *theodicy*, arguing that we live in the "best of all possible worlds," a concept lampooned in Voltaire's *Candide*, which, as noted above, acts as a cynical update to the book of Job.

Some Theological, Pastoral, and Ethical Implications

drawn to the book in the first place, often either conclude that Job is not a proper theodicy or posit a modified definition of *theodicy*.

If we were to conclude based on the book itself that we suffer because of some divine wager between God and Satan, we ignore the basis of the wager itself—that God offers Job to *hassatan* because "there is none like" Job on earth. That is, because of Job's singularity, one cannot identify with Job in a way that could offer one an explanation on one's own suffering since Job's suffering stems from his being unique.

Further into the book, the only explanations for Job's suffering we encounter are from Job's friends. Neither Yahweh nor the narrator explains anything to Job or to readers about the origins of suffering. In the medieval era, both Jewish and Christian Aristotelian scholars viewed the book of Job as a dialogue wherein Elihu offers the most lucid explanation of suffering vis-à-vis a sound understanding of providence. Saadiah Gaon (862–942), for instance, views Elihu as the unchallenged teacher who explains that all things work according to God's plan. Job's silence at the end of Elihu's speech is the ultimate reason that God addresses Job. God finds it necessary to "exhort [Job] to acknowledge Elihu's arguments and leave behind his fancies and suppositions."[4]

If one follows Saadiah, Maimonides, Calvin and others and turns to Elihu as the best expositor of the origin

---

4. Sa'adiah, *Book of Theodicy*, 414. Maimonides and Aquinas are similarly interested in providence in their interpretations of Job and are similarly Aristotelian, though Aquinas is less dependent on Elihu as a hero figure. See Yaffe, "Providence in Medieval Aristotelianism." Further, see John Calvin, who follows Aquinas in his sermons on Job, particularly Aquinas's reading of Job as teaching about providence and immortality, but resurrects (so to speak) Elihu as most important interlocutor. Schreiner, "'Why Do the Wicked Live?,'" 133–35.

of suffering, he or she could accept Elihu's explanation in 33:19 that sufferers "are chastened with pain upon their beds." But is this a definitive explanation for suffering? Even Elihu himself admits that "God speaks in one way, / and in two, though people do not perceive it" (33:14). What good is the chastening pain if one cannot perceive its motive? In the end, Elihu does not much justify the existence of innocent suffering. Rather, he justifies concluding that one may not know the origin of innocent suffering, which could be comforting for some.

There is also a hint at the end of Yahweh's second speech, when Yahweh does not admit to creating Leviathan, but merely contains the primordial beast. Thus, evil comes from outside of God's reign, and God in fact promises to slay the dragon on our behalf.[5] Whatever the proper theology of evil, the book of Job is surely less helpful than many people desire it to be. So what does Job say about suffering?

In 1791 Immanuel Kant wrote a small treatise titled "On the Miscarriage of all Philosophical Trials in Theodicy,"[6] which challenges all attempts at explaining the existence of evil in a God-created world. There are three problems that go against the purposes of God's wisdom, Kant reasons—sin, pain, and the disproportion of crime and punishment. These problems are typically explained away as "violations only against human wisdom" and not divine wisdom, as problems that could not be prevented by God, or as problems that stem from humanity such that "no guilt may be ascribed to God, for God has merely tolerated it."[7] Because all of these explanations fail to satisfy, Kant proposes what he calls "authentic theodicy," an example

---

5. See Levenson, *Creation and the Persistence of Evil*, 49; and Ortlund, "Identity of Leviathan."

6. Kant, "On the Miscarriage of All Philosophical Trials."

7. Ibid., 26–27.

Some Theological, Pastoral, and Ethical Implications

of which he finds in the book of Job. "Authentic theodicy," though, does not look much like traditional theodicy, for it does not do much to answer the question of why innocent people suffer. Rather, it points to the sufferer and his or her posture towards the suffering and toward God.

Kant argues that the book of Job provides us an allegory where one depends less on "subtle reasoning than on sincerity in taking notice of the impotence of our reason."[8] The book of Job describes a scene in which the friends attempt to understand or explain the reason for Job's suffering while Job "admits having hastily spoken about things which are too high for him and which he does not understand."[9] God justifies Job because of his honesty in his doubts over and against his friends' religious flattery.

Kant's short interpretation of Job typifies many conclusions of how Job may or may not respond to innocent suffering. If we are to take the book at its word, where God is an authoritative respondent and Job's friends are condemned for not speaking right about God, then surely it is significant to viewing or not viewing Job as theodicy that God never attempts to explain to Job why Job suffers, and that Job's friends do.

In the last chapter, I quote David Burrell from his book *Deconstructing Theodicy: Why The Book of Job Has Nothing to Say to the Puzzle of Suffering*. It is worth noting that the subtitle of Burrell's book is a bit misleading, for he admits that Job is not "useless for addressing the issues of undeserved suffering at the hands of a creator-God" but "that it rather directs us to eschew *explanation* for yet other ways of rendering enigmas intelligible."[10] Like Kant, Burrell sees the book of Job crediting Job for, if not honesty, exactly, then

8. Ibid., 34.
9. Ibid., 33.
10. Burrell, *Deconstructing Theodicy*, 123.

the direction of Job's speech *toward* God. The friends flatter and explain and defend while Job participates in a relationship. Though it may not seem like a friendly relationship, Job's confrontation with God presages encounter with God that Job's friends seem uninterested in. God rewards Job with some harsh words, but they are words directed back at Job.

No matter, says mid-century Swiss Old Testament scholar Wilhelm Vischer, for Job himself has expressed such a desire. In chapter 19, Job blames God for all his ills—physical, social, and spiritual—yet completes the chapter with an expression of faith that after his skin is destroyed, he will see God. Vischer, playing with the words and philosophy of Nietzsche, clarifies this ostensible conflict as Job's desiring "not goods, not the thing which is good; he lives of God's goodness which is beyond good and evil."[11]

JOB AFTER THE HOLOCAUST

Some may find such readings of Job frustrating, especially considering the places from which these writers are writing. Vischer, who wrote his work on Job in Germany during the run up to World War II, would eventually be exiled to Switzerland for his vocal opposition to National Socialism. But one would certainly consider that a pleasant fate compared to the fate of his Jewish peers. The Holocaust has inspired many to reconsider Job in the last century. A full analysis of the different approaches is beyond the scope of a small book such as this, but it is worth touching on a few different views on the subject.

First, it is natural for those who experienced the holocaust to be drawn to Job, for just as Job's trials have nothing to do with his guilt or innocence, so the suffering the Jews

11. Vischer, "Witness of Job to Jesus Christ," 42.

Some Theological, Pastoral, and Ethical Implications

of central Europe experienced in the 1930s and 1940s also had nothing to do with their guilt or lack thereof. One cannot pin their losses and pain to anything they did. Because the book of Job is a Jewish book, it should be one of the first places one would expect Jews to turn. Is there any particular part of the book of Job that speaks to those responding to the Shoah? Yes and no.

For Harold Kushner, who sees the Holocaust as a reason people have turned to the book of Job in recent years, the answers Job inspires are dependent on the historical-critical claim that the book of Job as we have it is the result of the redaction of multiple sources. The prose fable, Kushner claims, waters down the book as it stands, and so we should focus only on the poem for the real meaning of Job. Kushner begins with the premise that three things must be true: God must be all-powerful, God must be all good, and that evil exists. How does Job help us hold all three of these seemingly contradictory statements together? Kushner determines that the "answer lie[s] hidden in God's second speech from the whirlwind, the Behemoth and Leviathan passage, and in Job's final seven words."[12] After creation, Kushner posits that "God designated two areas of creation over which He would cede control. One was the domain of Nature and natural law." "God is moral," Kushner explained to citizens of New Orleans after Hurricane Katrina, "Nature is not."[13] The other area God ceded control of was "the human freedom to choose between good and evil."[14] These limitations are at work both in the book of Job and in the Holocaust. The Sabeans stole Job's cattle, choosing crime over goodness. The wind destroyed Job's children because Nature is blind. The speech on Leviathan is God's

12. Kushner, *Book of Job*, 196.
13. Ibid., 197.
14. Ibid., 198.

way of explaining Nature's amorality. Job's response, that he "repudiate[s his] past accusations," is a way of saying, "I know that I am not alone . . . and . . . I am comforted."[15] Job's response is an expression of his resilience also found in the survivors of the Holocaust, who remarried and created new families after their first families perished at the hands of the Nazis.[16] As we have seen, Job works, not as a way to explain suffering, but as a witness to the enduring relationship between a good God and a broken world.

For Elie Wiesel, all the many different parts of the book of Job that we have explored seem to have spoken to him over the decades since his survival of Auschwitz. Contra Kushner, Wiesel finds no comfort in Job's repentance. Wiesel has to imagine a different ending for the book of Job—one that is lost. Either that, or we should chose to read Job's confession as pretension only uttered to receive mercy from the God who has tortured him.[17]

At the beginning of the same essay, Wiesel admits to identifying strongly with Job. "We know [Job's] history for having lived it," he writes, "whenever we attempt to tell our own story, we transmit his."[18] Such allegorization of the text of Job in one's own life is common for those who suffer,

---

15. Ibid., 202.

16. As I mentioned above, Kushner rejects the prose fable as inferior to the poem, but Kushner's interpretation of Job fits rather nicely with other readings that accept the received text. Consider another recent response to the Holocaust vis-à-vis Job, where Alexander Goldberg writes, "If we can find the strength to reaffirm G-d, to question our ways of life and shed the arrogance of surety, then we can like Job rebuild our lives, our communities, our institutions." Goldberg, "Book of Job, Part 4." Goldberg here cites God's command to the friends to reconcile with Job and have Job pray for them, referring to the prose epilogue.

17. Wiesel, "Job: Our Contemporary," 232–35.

18. Ibid., 211–12.

Some Theological, Pastoral, and Ethical Implications

but Wiesel seems to embody the character of Job more than most. As one of the most important voices among Holocaust survivors, he kept returning to Job for a deeper understanding of his experience in Auschwitz and, like Job, his response changes over time—from doubt in God's justice to rebellion to silent acceptance. In a more recent essay, Wiesel again identifies with Job and admits to backing down from his protest, accepting that "there is a time for protest and a time for restraint, a time for memory and a time for forgiveness, a time for rebellion and a time for penitence."[19]

Again, Job does not offer explanation of suffering, but those who suffer are still drawn to him. One might expect someone like a cancer patient to look for explanation for their suffering in the book of Job, and finding no help there set Job aside for something else. Certainly some have done such a thing. But others cannot discard Job, despite the silence that comes after Yahweh's quizzical response from the tempest. Perhaps they are attracted to the character of Job, who feels free to protest the great Yahweh and, despite the tempestuous response, is declared right in the end because of his speech. There may be something to the freedom Job feels to confront God that is attractive to some. For other writers, though, it is less the confrontation than the freedom itself that is at the heart of Job.

THE FREEDOM OF GOD AND THE FREEDOM OF HUMANITY TO WORSHIP THAT GOD

If one were to expect an honest book on how Job responds to the innocent suffering, who better to provide it than Gustavo Gutiérrez? Gutiérrez spent his long career as a

---

19. Wiesel, "Job (1998)," 134, quoted in Larrimore, *Book of Job*, 227.

priest caring for and writing about the poor in Lima, Peru. Given his standing as the most prominent liberation theologian of the twentieth century, one would expect his book *On Job: God-Talk and the Suffering of the Innocent* to offer an "authentic theodicy." What one finds, however, is that Gutiérrez's book, though obviously concerned about innocent suffering, does not answer the question as a theodicy "should."

Job, according to Gutiérrez, is not even about theodicy or how to justify God in the face of suffering. Rather, it is about theology, or how to *talk about* God in the face of suffering. These are related, for theodicy is certainly a type of theology, strictly speaking, but Job shows us that the way one talks about God in the midst of suffering is not to justify the suffering. That, after all, is what the friends do. On the subject of the speech from the tempest, Gutiérrez writes:

> God assails the pretended knowledge of Job and even more than that of his friends, who regard everything as foreseen and think they know for certain when and how God has punished sinners. What God is criticizing here is every theology that presumes to pigeonhole the divine action in history and gives the illusory impression of knowing it in advance . . . God will bring [Job] to see that nothing, not even the world of justice, can shackle God.[20]

The language of theodicy too often devolves into a system with which one can hope to "manage . . . God's action."[21] Definitively answering why one suffers gives one a strategy to mitigate or eliminate that suffering in the future. It takes away God's freedom, but it also systematizes the hu-

20. Gutiérrez, *On Job*, 72.
21. Ibid., 75.

Some Theological, Pastoral, and Ethical Implications

man experience. The book of Job, as matter of fact, is not only about the freedom of God, but about the freedom of the individual in relationship with God.

In fact, narratively, the sufferings of Job stem from *hassatan* doubting Job's freedom. He claims that God has put a hedge around Job and that Job likely serves God because of that protection. The question for *hassatan* and Yahweh in the heavenly court is not about the problem of evil in the world but about whether there is such a thing as disinterested piety: Does Job serve God for no reason (*ḥinnām*)? The theme continues as the friends debate from a corollary position: Would God punish Job for no reason? In Job 9:17, Job's words point back to the initial question and foreshadow the theophany from the tempest (*səʿārâ*): "For he crushes me with a tempest (*səʿārâ*) and multiplies my wounds without cause (*ḥinnām*)."

Job's words seem harsh to his friends, but also subsequent readers of the book may find Job's words unfair because these readers know that Job is justified in the end. What we realize is the truth in the paradox of Job's existence, which testifies to Job's freedom found in true relationship with God. Job "would not have been obedient," declares Karl Barth, "if he had not raised this complaint and carried it through to the bitter end in spite of all objections."[22] Job's protest against God is a much clearer picture of devotion to the divine than any of his friends' sycophancy. I believe it is also more comforting to the afflicted than most traditional theodicies.

I cannot speak from my own experience since I have not suffered in a way analogous to how Job suffered, but I was struck in one particular instance during the Bible study I mentioned in the introduction. For one night per week over two months, after the community meal at the Servants

---

22. Barth, *CD* IV/3.1, 406.

to the Urban Poor in my neighborhood in Vancouver, I and the group read through the book of Job. I was interested in hearing how the book spoke to those who had been rendered homeless or addicted or trafficked or otherwise marginalized in what has been called the "most livable city in the world." Such circumstances can make people feel particularly outside the system in which many of us live. After reading through the complaint in chapter 3, which so offended Job's friends, my reading partners had a variety of responses. Several were offended along with Elphaz and Bildad, thinking Job overstepped some bounds of propriety. Another viewed Job as haunted by his own demons. Others identified with Job almost ashamedly. "I left a man who beat me," said one woman, "but I never wanted to die. . . I just ended up downtown on dope." "I can sound like Job, sometimes," said another, ". . . anger, jealousy, discouragement." One woman eventually spoke up after sitting in silence for a while. "I'm thankful for this," she said. "It doesn't make me feel so alone."

Job does not solve the problem of innocent suffering, but he joins others in solidarity through his free relationship with God. A few weeks later in that Bible study, after having read through the majority of the dialogues, we read through chapter 30 in Job's final defense. One woman spoke up after reading through the chapter: "I need to learn to complain like Job!" The participants were mainly Christians, steadfast in their devotion to God, but sometimes reticent to lament too loudly because of the milquetoast conventions the Western church has often established for fear of offending God or worse, in order to "reinforce and consolidate the political-economic monopoly of the status quo."[23] Job's freedom to complain and lament proves his devotion to the God who crushes him with a tempest.

23. Brueggemann, "Costly Loss of Lament," 102.

Some Theological, Pastoral, and Ethical Implications

It exhibits an "authentic theodicy" where philosophical theodicies fail. In writing about the lament psalms, Walter Brueggemann argues that the loss of lament signals the loss of "genuine covenant interaction."[24] By refusing to lament like the psalmists, one discounts the omnipotence of God along with God's concern for justice. Lament psalms like 22, 39, and 88, which address God and complain about God, model the type of petition we as believers are expected to invoke. The book of Job models such complaints over a sustained period through the voice of a particular character. Job's freedom in his lamentation offers us a model of free faith.

Such a faith is risky for it demands a response and confrontation with the omnipotent God in whom Job claims to believe. When Yahweh does finally respond to Job, God does not mention Job's sufferings explicitly but describes only his own creativity. Though there is plenty of evidence (described in previous chapters) that the speech from the tempest works as a restoration of Job's de-creative speech in chapter 3, one must still be struck by the elements of creation that Yahweh chooses to invoke. I will speak more about creation below, but apropos to the topic of divine freedom, note that the animals especially are primarily wild animals. They are, in most cases, either useless (mountain goats), dangerous (lions), or ridiculous (the ostrich) to humans. These animals' wildness reflects the kind of deity that would think to create them. Yahweh is a free god with plans that befit such a free god.

The resulting narrative, then, does not act as a traditional theodicy, because the question of evil is incidental to the narrative. Job's sufferings act merely as a vehicle for exploring the larger question of human and divine freedom. Of course, as we have seen above, the book of Job can still

24. Ibid., 102.

aid one in confronting evil or profound suffering. But perhaps one should approach such a subject through the lens of divine and human freedom.[25]

Gutiérrez sees the divine speeches as exemplifying God's freedom, and by implication the true power of God's love. Because even justice cannot shackle God, we know that God is truly free. "God's love is a cause," Gutiérrez explains, "not an effect that is, as it were, handcuffed."[26] Such a freedom of God's love encourages an interpersonal ethic among God's free people. Gutiérrez follows Job's own theological development from unbridled complaint in chapter 3 through the arguments with his friends who hold fast to a theology Job once held himself and to Job's final defense in chapters 29–31 where he recognizes the plight of those in a worse state than he. This is the moment Job hears from Elihu and Yahweh—when he sees the world through the eyes of the poor. "The solidarity with the poor and the starving, which leads to an ongoing transformation of history and requires behavior to this end, is the fruit of the gratuitous love of . . . God."[27]

When Job and Yahweh meet at that tempest, Gutiérrez calls it the "mysterious meeting of two freedoms."[28] That mysteriousness is an important aspect of the story for it encourages identification with Job in one's own sufferings, which has been born out in the history of the interpretation of Job. Job's free relationship with Yahweh does not hamstring him to a particular time or antiquated problems. Job is our contemporary because he is timeless.

---

25. This is something Kushner eventually does even though he is drawn to Job because of his own sufferings and because Job is a "good person" to whom "bad things [have] happened."

26. Gutiérrez, *On Job*, 73.

27. Ibid., 99.

28. Ibid., 67.

Some Theological, Pastoral, and Ethical Implications

CREATION

According to Genesis 1, on the sixth day of creation, God created humans and commanded them to "be fruitful and multiply, fill the earth and subdue it." According to many critics of Christian theology, most famously, Lynn White, this first divine commandment to humans has led to our current ecological crisis.[29] There is, perhaps, some truth to White's claim despite protests from environmentally sensitive exegetes.[30] The primacy of the creation story in Genesis 1 would certainly lead many to conclude its primacy as an ethic, and less sophisticated exegetes might conclude that such a command gives humanity license to dominate the earth with little concern for its ecology. Furthermore, that the Bible begins with Genesis 1 must mean to many that it is the most important creation text. The problem for many readers of the Bible is that there are other biblical texts that recount the creation of the world by God, and creation often looks quite different in those accounts. That should not cancel out the command to subdue the earth (whatever that might mean), but it might limit the command somewhat, depending on one's hermeneutic.

The book of Job, for instance, offers a mitigating vision of the creation story despite displaying an awareness of the Priestly creation text from Genesis 1. First, note that the narrator's description of Job portrays him as one who has, in fact, been fruitful and multiplied. He has, after all, seven sons and three daughters, which is a large number of children in any era. Job also has demonstrated his willingness to exercise dominion over things that move upon the earth, such as his large cache of livestock (seven thousand

---

29. White, "The Historical Roots of Our Ecological Crisis," 1203–7.

30. See Provan, *Seriously Dangerous Religion*, 32.

sheep, three thousand camels, five hundred yoke of oxen, five hundred donkeys).[31]

Furthermore, when Job opens his mouth to curse his day in chapter 3, he certainly parodies Gen 1:4's "Let there be light" by saying "that day, let there be darkness." What follows, as we noted in the previous chapter, is a metaphorical dismantling of creation. So when God responds from the tempest, and specifically responds in chapter 38 to Job's opening speech from chapter 3, the author of Job is not merely offering a new, independent creation narrative. Rather, God's speech is informed by Genesis 1.

There is nothing inherently problematic with two creation narratives, obviously—for the distinct creation narrative focusing on the garden of Eden in Genesis 2 follows the seven-day creation narrative of Gen 1:1—2:3. What the creation text of Job does, however, is not solely augment the Priestly text (as some might suggest Genesis 2 does to Genesis 1), but rather it offers a competing thesis of creation and humanity's role in it. God does not tell Job from the tempest that Job is to fill the earth and subdue it, nor is Job called to till it and keep it (Gen 2:15). Rather, Job is told that he is not at all instrumental in the work of creation or its maintenance. The sarcasm in God's rhetorical questions throughout the speeches indicates that Job evidently knows how far-flung the universe is and how incidental to it humanity is.[32]

The theological point of the speeches from the tempest does not, however, promote a theology that demotes

---

31. See Meier, "Job I–II: A Reflection," 183–93.

32. Job's own speech in 7:17–21 and elsewhere suggests that he already knows his insignificance in the world. Humanity's transience, in fact, is one of his reasons for questioning the justice of his suffering. "What does my punishment accomplish," he seems to be saying, "considering my insignificance in the grand scheme of things."

Some Theological, Pastoral, and Ethical Implications

humanity as just another animal, particularly when the speeches are coupled with the restoration of Job in the epilogue. That God, even after speaking of all the nooks and crannies of creation with no bearing on Job's life, deigns to restore Job and even call him "my servant" shows that God does, in fact, hold humanity in a high regard—as a servant of God and a servant of God's creation.

What, then, should we take from this conclusion? What is the proper ethic promoted here if a lowly human can still be considered a servant of God and creation? As a test case, let us consider the forest and our relationship with it.

As far back as the Elizabethan era, people have been concerned with human exploitation of the forests, though there was little knowledge of the importance of the forests to ecology across the globe. John Manwood, a jurist and gamekeeper of the Waltham Forest, wrote a treatise on the laws of the forest in 1592 in England, defining a forest as a "certain territory of woody grounds and fruitful pastures, privileged for wild beasts and fowls of forest, chase, and warren, to rest and abide there in the safe protection of the king, for his delight and pleasure."[33] In other words, a forest is a forest if it is a sanctuary for wildlife and nothing more (other than the delight of the king).

By the Enlightenment, however, Europeans' understanding of forests had changed, and the forest was defined not as a space for wildlife or even as a place of "delight and pleasure." Rather, the forest became a space that could keep the economy strong. Robert Pogue Harrison, who writes about the evolution of the European understanding of forests in *Forests: The Shadow of Civilization*, marks the change in attitude with Monsieur Le Roy's eighteenth-century

33. Manwood, *Treatise of the Laws of the Forest*; cited in Harrison, *Forests*, 72.

Encyclopédie entry on "forest." The key terms in the entry are "public interest" and "public utility," which reduce the woods to humanity's economic interests. Le Roy writes, "Religion itself had consecrated forests, doubtlessly to protect, through veneration, that which had to be conserved for the public interest."[34] As we have seen, this understanding, even in the case of religion, contradicts Yahweh's speech to Job from the tempest. There is no sense in the book of Job that Job or anyone should find the ostrich useful at all. Yahweh's point is that the ostrich "forgets wisdom," and yet it remains mysteriously important to Yahweh despite its seeming ridiculousness. But the Enlightenment understanding of forests as public utility has remained and even influenced those who wish to preserve the forest, for religious reasons or otherwise. Harrison explains:

> The Manwoodians of today are forced, however, to speak the language of those whom they oppose. This is precisely the language of usefulness. In their efforts to preserve the forest sanctuaries, they must remind science as well as governments that one day the abundant diversity of plant species that exist nowhere else but in the forests will prove useful and beneficial for such things as treating cancer or other diseases. They must contrive a thousand convincing or unconvincing arguments in favor of the utility of forest conservation.[35]

As we learn more about forests, it becomes difficult for readers not to hear the voice from the tempest reminding us of our own irrelevance with respect to the forest. That is, the tables have been turned. We want to help the forests as they have helped us, but one of the only things we can

---

34. Cited in Harrison, *Forests*, 115.
35. Ibid., 124.

Some Theological, Pastoral, and Ethical Implications

do is respect them. Consider some of the forests in North America near where I am writing this. In the case of the edenic old growth Douglas-fir canopies and the rich biodiversity therein, the only real way that one can "till them and keep them" (in Hebrew, "to serve them and protect them") is to put a hedge around them and let them be. One of the thousands of organisms that live and grow in the Douglas-fir canopy is the lichen *Lobaria oregana*, which botanists have recently discovered are extremely slow-growing producers of massive amounts of nitrogen. The amount of nitrogen the Lobaria provides the forest depends on the age of the Lobaria, which is dependent on the age of the trees in which they live. In fact, Lobaria of any size may not be found in Douglas firs younger than two hundred years old. Even then, it will take another three hundred years for the Lobaria to produce the nitrogen that will most benefit the ecosystem. Furthermore, there is nothing we can do to speed up the process.[36] The *Lobaria oregana*, and the Douglas firs upon which they grow, need what God can give it and that a single generation of humanity cannot—time. In other words, the best thing we can do for the forest is respect its place in God's creation.

Note the challenge that arises when even discussing the theology of creation in the book of Job. We can discuss the importance of old growth, temperate rain forests to humanity—how the huge amount of carbon stored in old growth trees is one of the most important mitigators of climate change in the world, and how important it is to the future of humanity to slow global warming by protecting forests—but then again, we introduce the language of "usefulness" into creation. The usefulness of creation to humanity is not even a factor in the theology of Job. In fact, the

36. Antoine, "Ecophysiological Approach." See also Preston, *Wild Trees*, 185–86.

introduction of utility brings us back to the pretheophany theology of Job and his friends. Though that language may aid us in our service to and protection of God's creation from humanity's oversubjugation of the earth, in the end we must remember the free God who brought it about and our insignificance and absence in that bringing. Even as we learn more about lichens and their role in the forest ecosystem, we still speak "by words without knowledge."

CONCLUSION

The book of Job ends as tidily as any book in the Bible. Job lives long enough to see four generations, and he dies old and content. Such an ending has not satisfied his readers though. We keep coming back to it, assuming there is more to find, and it has yet to disappoint. As a character from Kierkegaard's novella *Repetition* says, "It is impossible to describe all the shades of meaning [of Job] and how manifold the meaning is that he has for me . . . Now a word by him arouses me from my lethargy and awakens new restlessness; now it calms the sterile raging within me, stops the dreadfulness in the mute nausea of my passion. Have you really read Job? Read him, read him again and again."[37] Kierkegaard wrote *Repetition* a century before the Holocaust and more than a century before our current ecological crisis, and yet we have seen how Job has spoken to those two events as well as it does to the personal existential issues for which Kierkegaard and others sought help.

We do not have the space to explore all the different areas that Job could help us to better understand. I pray this companion satisfies as a foray into the book of Job, recognizing that it cannot approach the final word on Job. I also pray that it is clear to readers that one must now go back

---

37. Kierkegaard, *Fear and Trembling / Repetition*, 204.

Some Theological, Pastoral, and Ethical Implications

and read Job from the beginning to discover how it might speak to individual readers in surprising ways, as it has to readers throughout its existence.

REVIEW QUESTIONS

1. How does the book of Job answer or not answer the problem of innocent suffering?
2. Gustavo Gutiérrez's book on Job has the subtitle, *God-Talk and the Suffering of the Innocent*. In short, Gutiérrez sees Job as almost a primer on how to do theology. How do you think Job might contribute to questions of "theological method," i.e., on how to talk about God?
3. If you were tasked with writing a sermon on the book of Job, what would be your main points?

WORKS CITED

Adams, Nicholas. "The Goodness of Job's Bad Arguments." *Journal of Scriptural Reasoning* 4/1 (2004). http://jsr.shanti.virginia.edu/back-issues/vol-4-no-1-july-2004-the-wisdom-of-job/the-goodness-of-jobs-bad-arguments/.

Alter, Robert. *The Art of Biblical Poetry*. New York: Basic, 1985.

———. *The Wisdom Books: Job, Proverbs, and Ecclesiastes*. New York: Norton, 2010.

Althann, Robert. "Reflections on the Text of the Book of Job." In *Sôfer Mahîr: Essays in Honour of Adrian Shenker*, edited by Yahanan A. P. Goldman et al., 7–13. Vetus Testamentum Supplements 110. Leiden: Brill, 2006.

Antoine, Marie E. "An Ecophysiological Approach to Quantifying Nitrogen Fixation By Lobaria Oregana." *Bryologist* 107 (2004) 82–87.

Barth, Karl. *Church Dogmatics*. Translated by G. W. Bromiley. Vol. IV/3.1, *The Doctrine of Reconciliation*, Part 3, First Half. Edited by G. W. Bromiley and T. F. Torrance. Edinburgh: T. & T. Clark, 1961.

Brueggemann, Walter. "The Costly Loss of Lament." In *The Psalms and the Life of Faith*, edited by Patrick D. Miller, 57–71. Minneapolis: Fortress, 1995.

Burrell, David. *Deconstructing Theodicy: Why Job Has Nothing to Say to the Puzzle of Suffering*. Grand Rapids: Brazos, 2008.

Caquot, André. "Le Léviathan de Job 40:25–41:26." *Revue Biblique* 99 (1992) 40–69.

Clines, David J. A. *Job 1–20*. Word Biblical Commentary 17. Waco, TX: Word, 1989.

———. *Job 21–37*. Word Biblical Commentary 18A. Nashville: Nelson, 2006.

———. "Putting Elihu in His Place: A Proposal for the Relocation of Job 32–37." *Journal for the Study of the Old Testament* 29 (2004) 243–53.

———. "Why Is There a Book of Job, and What Does It Do to You If You Read it?" In *The Book of Job*, edited by W. A. M. Beuken, 1–20. Bibliotheca Ephemeridum theologicarum Lovaniensium 114. Leuven: Leuven University Press, 1994.

Cox, Claude. "'*Ipsissima Verba*': The Translator's 'Actual Words' in Old Greek Job and What They Tell Us about the Translator and the Nature of the Translation." Paper presented at the International Organization for Septuagint and Cognate Studies session at the Annual Meeting of the Society of Biblical Literature. Atlanta, November 21–24, 2015.

Dhorme, E. *A Commentary on the Book of Job*. Translated by Harold Knight. London: Nelson, 1967.

Driver, S. R., and George Buchanan Gray. *A Critical and Exegetical Commentary on the Book of Job: Together with a New Translation*. International Critical Commentary. Edinburgh: T. & T. Clark, 1921.

Fokkelman, J. P. *The Book of Job in Form: A Literary Translation with Commentary*. Translated by Jan P. Fokkelman. Studia Semitica Neerlandica 58. Leiden: Brill, 2012.

Goldberg, Alexander. "The Book of Job, Part 4: Theodicy on 'Planet Auschwitz.'" *The Guardian* 19 July 2010. http://www.theguardian.com/commentisfree/belief/2010/jul/16/job-theodicy-religion-judaism/.

Gordis, Robert. *The Book of God and Man: A Study of Job*. Chicago: University of Chicago Press, 1965.

———. *The Book of Job: Commentary, New Translation, and Special Studies*. Moreshet Series 2. New York: Jewish Theological Seminary of America, 1978.

Gregory I, Pope. *Morals on the Book of Job*. 3 vols. in 4 books. 1844. Reprinted, Eugene, OR: Wipf & Stock, 2013.

Gutiérrez, Gustavo. *On Job: God-Talk and the Suffering of the Innocent*. Translated by Matthew J. O'Connell. Maryknoll, NY: Orbis, 1987.

Habel, Norman C. *The Book of Job: A Commentary*. Old Testament Library. Philadelphia: Westminster, 1985.

Harris, R. Laird. "The Book of Job and Its Doctrine of God." *Grace Theological Journal* 13 (1972) 3–33.

Harrison, Robert Pogue. *Forests: The Shadow of Civilization*. Chicago: University of Chicago Press, 1992.

Works Cited

Hartley, John E. *The Book of Job*. New International Commentary on the Old Testament. Grand Rapids: Eerdmans, 1988.

Holman, Jan. "Does My Redeemer Live or Is My Redeemer the Living God? Some Reflections on the Translation of Job 19,25." In *The Book of Job*, edited by W. A. M. Beuken, 377–81. Bibliotheca Ephemeridum theologicarum Lovaniensium 114. Leuven: Leuven University Press, 1994.

Janzen, J. Gerald. *Job*. Interpretation. Atlanta: John Knox, 1985.

Kafka, Franz. *The Trial*. Translated by Willa and Edwin Muir. New York: Schocken, 1956.

Kaminsky, Joel S. "Would You Impugn My Justice? A Nuanced Approach to the Hebrew Bible's Theology of Divine Recompense." *Interpretation* 69 (2015) 299–310.

Kant, Immanuel. "On the Miscarriage of All Philosophical Trials in Theodicy." In *Religion and Rational Theology*, edited by Allen W. Wood and George di Giovanni, 21–37. Cambridge Edition of the Works of Immanuel Kant. Cambridge: Cambridge University Press, 2001.

Kierkegaard, Søren. *Eighteen Upbuilding Discourses*. Translated by Howard V. Hong and Edna H. Hong. Kierkegaard's Writings 5. Princeton: Princeton University Press, 1990.

———. *Fear and Trembling / Repetition*. Translated by Howard V. Hong and Edna H. Hong. Kierkegaard's Writings 6. Princeton: Princeton University Press, 1983.

Kushner, Harold S. *The Book of Job: When Bad Things Happened to a Good Person*. Jewish Encounters Series. New York: Nextbook, 2012.

Kuyper, L. J. "The Repentance of Job." *Vetus Testamentum* 9 (1959) 91–94.

Larrimore, Mark. *The Book of Job: A Biography*. Lives of Great Religious Books. Princeton: Princeton University Press, 2013.

Lawrie, Douglas. "How Critical Is It to Be Historically Critical? The Case of the Composition of the Book of Job." *Journal of Northwest Semitic Languages* 27 (2001) 121–46.

Levenson, Jon. *Creation and the Persistence of Evil: The Jewish Drama of Divine Omnipotence*. San Francisco: Harper & Row, 1988.

Lévêque, Jean. "L'Interprétation des Discours de Yhwh (Job 38,1–42,6)." In *The Book of Job*, edited by W. A. M. Beuken, 203–22. Bibliotheca Ephemeridum theologicarum Lovaniensium 114. Leuven: Leuven University Press, 1994.

Longman, Tremper, III. *Job*. Baker Commentary on the Old Testament Wisdom and Psalms. Grand Rapids: Baker Academic, 2012.

Works Cited

MacLeish, Archibald. *J. B.: A Play in Verse*. Boston: Houghton Mifflin, 1958.

Maimonides. *The Guide of the Perplexed*. Translated by Chaim Rabin. New York: East and West Library, 1947.

Meier, Sam. "Job I–II: A Reflection of Genesis I–III." *Vetus Testamentum* 39 (1989) 183–93.

Michel, Walter L. "Confidence and Despair: Job 19,25–27 in the Light of Northwest Semitic Studies." In *The Book of Job*, edited W. A. M. Beuken, 157–81. Bibliotheca Ephemeridum theologicarum Lovaniensium 114. Leuven: Leuven University Press, 1994.

Murphy, Roland E. *The Tree of Life: An Exploration of Biblical Wisdom Literature*. 3rd ed. Grand Rapids: Eerdmans, 2002.

Nelson, Alissa Jones. "Justice and Biblical Interpretation beyond Subjectivity and Self-Determination: A Contrapuntal Reading on the Theme of Suffering in the Book of Job." *Political Theology* 11 (2010) 431–52.

Neusner, Jacob, trans. *Baba Batra*. Chicago Studies in the History of Judaism 30. Chicago: University of Chicago Press, 1984.

Newsom, Carol A. *The Book of Job: A Contest of Moral Imaginations*. Oxford: Oxford University Press, 2003.

Ortlund, Eric. "The Identity of Leviathan and the Meaning of the Book of Job." *Trinity Journal* 34 (2013) 17–30.

Patrick, Dale. "The Translation of Job XLII 6." *Vetus Testamentum* 26 (1976) 369–71.

Petersen, Michael J. "Job 28: The Theological Center of the Book of Job." PhD diss., Bob Jones University, 1994.

Pope, Marvin H. *Job: Introduction, Translation, and Notes*. 3rd ed. The Anchor Bible 15. Garden City, NY: Doubleday, 1973.

Porter, Stanley E. "The Message of the Book of Job: Job 42:7b as Key to Interpretation?" *Evangelical Quarterly* 63 (1991) 291–304.

Preston, Richard. *The Wild Trees: A Story of Passion and Daring*. New York: Random House, 2008.

Provan, Iain. *Seriously Dangerous Religion: What the Old Testament Really Says and Why It Matters*. Waco: Baylor University Press, 2014.

Rowley, H. H. *Job*. New Century Bible. Greenwood, SC: Attic, 1976.

Sa'adia ben Joseph. *The Book of Theodicy: A Translation and Commentary on the Book of Job*. Translated by L. E. Goodman. Yale Judaica Series. New Haven: Yale University Press, 1988.

Schreiner, Susan E. *Where Shall Wisdom Be Found? Calvin's Exegesis of Job from Medieval and Modern Perspectives*. Chicago: University of Chicago Press, 1994.

Works Cited

———. "'Why Do the Wicked Live?': Job and David in Calvin's Sermons on Job." In *The Voice from the Whirlwind: Interpreting the Book of Job*, edited by Leo G. Perdue and Clark Gilpin, 129–43. Nashville: Abingdon, 1992.

Seitz, Christopher. "The Patience of Job in the Epistle of James." *Konsequente Traditionsgeschichte* (1993) 373–82.

Seow, C. L. "Elihu's Revelation." *Theology Today* 68 (2011) 253–71.

———. *Job 1–21: Interpretation and Commentary*. Illuminations. Grand Rapids: Eerdmans, 2013.

Syring, Wolf-Dieter. *Hiob und Sein Anwalt: Die Prosatext des Hiobbuches und Ihre Rolle in Seiner Redaktions- und Rezeptionsgechichte*. Beihefte zur Zeitschrift für die alttestamentliche Wissenschaft 336. Berlin: de Gruyter, 1993.

Terrien, Samuel L. *Job: Poet of Existence*. 1957. Reprinted, Eugene, OR: Wipf & Stock, 2004.

Thomas Aquinas, Saint. *The Literal Exposition on Job: A Scriptural Commentary Concerning Providence*. Translated by Anthony Damico. Classics in Religious Studies 7. Atlanta: Scholars, 1989.

Timmer, Daniel. "God's Speeches, Job's Responses, and the Problem of Coherence in the Book of Job: Sapiential Pedagogy Revisited." *Catholic Biblical Quarterly* 71 (2009) 286–305.

Vicchio, Stephen J. *Job in the Ancient World*. Image of the Biblical Job: A History. Eugene, OR: Wipf & Stock, 2006.

———. *Job in the Medieval World*. Image of the Biblical Job: A History. Eugene, OR: Wipf & Stock, 2006.

———. *Job in the Modern World*. Image of the Biblical Job: A History. Eugene, OR: Wipf & Stock, 2006.

Vischer, Wilhelm. "The Witness of Job to Jesus Christ." *Evangelical Quarterly* 48 (1934) 40–53.

———. "The Witness of Job to Jesus Christ." *Evangelical Quarterly* 48 (1934) 138–50.

Walton, John H. with Kelly Vizcaino. *Job: From Biblical Text . . . to Contemporary Life*. NIV Application Commentary. Grand Rapids: Zondervan, 2012.

White, Lynn. "The Historical Roots of Our Ecological Crisis." *Science* 155 (1967) 1203–7.

Wiesel, Elie. "Job: Our Contemporary." In *Messengers of God: Biblical Portraits and Legends*, 211–35. New York: Simon & Schuster, 1976.

———. *The Trial of God (as It Was Held on February 25, 1649, in Shamgorod): A Play*. Translated by Marion Wiesel. New York: Schocken, 1995.

Works Cited

Wolde, Ellen van. "Job 42,1–6: The Reversal of Job." In *The Book of Job*, edited by W. A. M. Beuken, 223–50. Bibliotheca Ephemeridum theologicarum Lovaniensium 114. Leuven: Leuven University Press, 1994.

Yaffe, Martin D. "Interpretive Essay." In *The Literal Exposition on Job*, by Saint Thomas Aquinas, 1–66. Classics in Religious Studies 7. Atlanta: Scholars, 1989.

———. "Providence in Medieval Aristotelianism: Moses Maimonides and Thomas Aquinas on the Book of Job." In *The Voice from the Whirlwind: Interpreting the Book of Job*, edited by Leo G. Perdue and W. Clark Gilpin, 111–28. Nashville: Abingdon, 1992.

Young, Edward J. *An Introduction to the Old Testament*. Grand Rapids: Eerdmans, 1964.

NAME INDEX

Adams, Nicholas, 78
Alter, Robert, 15, 37, 50, 58–59, 95
Althann, Robert, 67
Antoine, Marie E., 129

Barth, Karl, 78, 87, 107, 121
Blake, William, 9
Brueggeman, Walter, 122
Burrell, David, 108, 115–16

Calvin, John, 77–78, 88, 113–14
Caquot, André, 97
Clines, David J. A., 3, 63, 86
Cox, Claude, 66–67

Dhorme, E., 59
Driver, S. R., 59

Fokkelman, J. P., 64, 66, 85–86, 101–2

Goldberg, Alexander, 118
Gordis, Robert, 21
Gray, George Buchanan, 59
Gregory I, Pope, 81–82, 111–12

Gutiérrez, Gustavo, 72–73, 119–21, 124

Habel, Norman C., 21, 64, 80, 91, 101–2, 105
Handel, George Frideric, 81
Harris, R. Laird, 55
Harrison, Robert Pogue, 127–28
Hartley, John E., 49
Hitler, Adolf, 110
Holman, Jan, 80

Janzen, J. Gerald, 21, 64, 65, 86
Jerome, 81

Kafka, Franz, 35, 111
Kaminsky, Joel S., 83–84
Kant, Immanuel, 112, 114–16
Kierkegaard, Søren, 74–75, 111, 130
Kushner, Harold S., 110, 117–19, 124
Kuyper, L. J., 101

Larrimore, Mark, 76, 119
Lawrie, Douglas, 61, 65
Leibniz, Gottfried, 112

Name Index

Le Roy, Monsieur, 127–28
Lévêque, Jean, 96
Levenson, Jon, 97, 114
Lo, Alison, 85
Longman, Tremper, III, 26, 84
Lowth, Robert, 55, 58–59

MacLeish, Archibald, 9, 76, 111
Maimonides, 76, 88, 90, 113–14
Malick, Terrence, 111
Manwood, John, 127–28
Meier, Sam, 38, 126
Michel, Walter L., 80
Milton, John, 27
Murphy, Roland E., 39

Nelson, Alyssa Jones, 78
Newsom, Carol A., 17, 21, 26, 36, 40, 59, 63, 77, 84, 87, 94
Nietzsche, Friedrich, 116

Ortlund, Eric, 97–98, 114

Patrick, Dale, 101
Paul, the Apostle, 77
Pope, Marvin, H., 25, 59, 62, 63

Porter, Stanley E., 106
Preston, Richard, 129
Provan, Iain, 125
Putin, Vladimir, 111
Rowley, H. H., 64

Sa'adia ben Joseph, 76, 88, 102–3, 113–14
Schreiner, Susan, 77, 88, 113
Seitz, Christopher R., 74
Seow, C. L., 26, 30, 35–36, 58, 64–66, 90

Terrien, Samuel L., 63
Thomas Aquinas, 76–78
Timmer, Daniel, 101

Vischer, Wilhelm, 116
Voltaire, 111–12

Walton, John, 65
White, Lynn, 125
Wiesel, Elie, 35, 91, 111, 118–19
Wolde, Ellen van, 99

Yaffe, Martin D., 76–77, 113
Young, Edward J., 55

Zviagintsev, Andrey, 111

ANCIENT DOCUMENT INDEX

OLD TESTAMENT/
HEBREW BIBLE

Genesis

1–50	54, 57
1	125–26
1:1—2:3	126
1:3	50, 57–58, 95
1:28	37
2:15	126
2:17	38
2:23	30
17:1–2	10, 48
25:8	49
29:14	30

Exodus

32:12	101
33:11	107

Numbers

22:22	28

Deuteronomy

19:6–12	36
25:7	35

Judges

9:2	30
21:6	101

Ruth

3:9–12	36

1 Samuel

1:1	25

2 Samuel

5:1	30
13:39	101

1 Chronicles

1–29	59
12:20	25
21:15	52
26:7	25

Ancient Document Index

1 Chronicles *(continued)*

27:18	25

2 Chronicles

1–36	59

Esther

1–10	59

Job

1–2	11, 28
1:1–3	42
1:1	16, 48
1:3	10
1:4–5	32
1:5	31, 41
1:6–12	35
1:7	12, 71
1:8	16–17, 71
1:9–11	71
1:9	11, 30, 71–73, 75
1:11	31
1:12	28
1:15	6, 33, 34
1:16	33
1:17	33
1:19	13, 33
1:21–22	16, 73–75
1:21	10, 15
1:22	71
2	65
2:1–6	35
2:3	12, 16–17
2:5	30, 31
2:7	29
2:8	48, 51, 52, 100, 102
2:9–10	71
2:9	29, 30
2:10	11, 29, 31
2:11–13	1
2:11	102
2:12	48, 51, 52, 102
3–41	44
3–31	103–4
3–27	75–78
3	15, 37, 50, 51, 52, 74, 85, 90, 94–95, 100, 126
3:1–26	94
3:1–2	28
3:2	11–12
3:3–4	55–56
3:3	57
3:4	50, 95
3:8	37, 97–98
3:11–12	55–56
3:23	95
4–5	18
4:3	23
4:4	20
4:6	20
4:8	18
4:12–16	26
4:12	47–48, 51
4:17	19
5	19, 40
5:8	40
5:13	77
5:17	23, 27
6:19	34
7	57–8
7:1	71
7:17–21	126
7:17–19	57–58
8	40, 75
8:4	32
8:5	40
8:6	23, 27
8:8–10	21
8:11–19	39
8:21–22	21–22
9	35
9:2	35

Ancient Document Index

Reference	Pages
9:17	30, 75, 121
9:21	100
10:2	35
11	40
11:13–15	40
11:14–21	23
12:9	15
13:6–8	35
15	18, 19
15:2–3	20
15:10	19
15:17–8	19
15:20	20
16:9ff.	105
16:17	41
16:19–22	80–81
16:19	35, 80
18:5–6	22
18:5	22
19	81, 116
19:7–12	79
19:12	81
19:13–20	79
19:17	30, 31, 56
19:23	79
19:24	56, 58
19:25–27	79–82
19:25	36, 79, 80, 81
19:26	80
20:4–5	23
21:7–20	56
22	18, 20, 40
22:1–30	63
22:6–9	20
22:22	40
23:1—24:17	63
23	35
23:1–7	77
24–27	62
24	63
24:12	41
24:18–24	63
24:25	63
25	22
25:1–6	63
25:6	22
26	62
26:1–4	63
26:5–14	63
27	24, 39, 63, 84
27:1–12	63
27:13–23	63
28–31	86
28	39–40, 48, 60, 63, 65, 82–87, 96
28:1–11	85
28:7–8	85
28:12–19	85
28:20–22	85
28:23–27	85
28:28	39–40, 86
29–31	35, 48, 93, 124
29	63, 84
29:4	93
29:7–25	42
29:9–10	93
29:12	10
29:15	10
30:19	48, 51, 93–94, 100, 102
31:9–10	10
31:10	30, 31
31:19	10
31:25–27	93
31:35	13
31:37	91
32–37	60, 64, 87–90
32	26
32:8	89
32:9	89
32:18	26, 89
33	26, 39
33:4	26

Job (continued)

33:6	89
33:8–11	89
33:14–15	87
33:14	114
33:19	89, 114
33:23–28	27
33:23	26, 89
33:28	89
35:6–8	90
36–37	26
36:3	89
36:4	26, 89
36:5	100
38–41	90–98, 104
38:1—39:30	13
38	12, 30, 96–97
38:2–5	91
38:2–3	92
38:2	13, 24–5, 94
38:3	89, 95
38:4–21	92
38:4–7	13, 19
38:4	37
38:7	95
38:8–11	13
38:8	95
38:9	95
38:12–21	13
38:19–20	95
38:22–38	92
38:22–31	13
38:22–25	95
38:26	95
38:31–33	13
38:39—39:30	92
38:39	95
39	14, 96–97
39:13–18	95
40–41	60, 66
40:2	24–25
40:3–5	96–97
40:4–5	27, 64, 103
40:4	93–94
40:6—41:34	13, 64
40:15—41:34	92
40:15–24	14
41	14
41:1–34	37
42	45, 70, 103
42:1–6	51, 98–103
42:1–5	99
42:2–6	27
42:5	80, 99
42:6–7	17, 22
42:6	48, 51, 52, 93–94, 99, 100–102
42:7–9	48, 50
42:7–8	2, 24–25, 41–42, 93, 103–8
42:7	80, 102
42:8–10	40–41
42:9	40–41
42:13	32
42:17	48

Psalms

1	82
8:4–5	57
22	123
37	82
39	123
88	123
119	82

Proverbs

1–31	38–39, 82, 83
8:22–36	38

Ecclesiastes

1–12	38–39, 82, 83

Ancient Document Index

Isaiah

1–66	56–57
29:21	35
30:12	52
32:6	107–8
57:6	52

Jeremiah

1–52	55–57
8:6	52
12:1–3	56
17:1	56
18:8	52
18:10	52
20:8	56
20:14–18	55–56
31:15	52, 101

Lamentations

1–5	56–57

Ezekiel

14	73
14:14	54
14:19	54
14:20	60

Joel

2:13	52

Amos

7:3	52
7:6	52

Jonah

3:10	52
4:2	52

Zechariah

3:1–2	28, 58

APOCRYPHA

Sirach

42:15—43:33	38

NEW TESTAMENT

1 Corinthians

3:19	77

James

5:11	73–74

RABBINIC WRITINGS

Babylonian Talmud

Baba Batra 14b	55

www.ingramcontent.com/pod-product-compliance
Lightning Source LLC
Chambersburg PA
CBHW022125160426
43197CB00009B/1155